Masao Takenaka

RECONCILIATION

AND RENEWAL IN JAPAN

Published jointly by the

Student Volunteer Movement

for Christian Missions

and Friendship Press, New York

275.2
T13

CONTENTS

22932

INTRODUCTION

We have, as Westerners, only in recent years begun to take seriously the existence of the Far East—a recognition that has been less the fruit of Christian convictions about the interdependence of men and nations before God than one that has been wrung from reluctant minds by the blood baths of the last two decades. We have become increasingly aware that a massive revolution is taking place in Asia in which long denied and restive peoples are in ferment; colonial yokes are being cast off; revolutionary ideas are in the air; and the fabric of ancient social structures is undergoing radical change. In seeking to comprehend the meaning and character of this revolution and our relation to it, we have also been awakened to the limitations of our understanding, the relativity of our perspective, and our need for correction and illumination by the perspectives of Christians in other lands. This book on Japan, written particularly for students in America by an able and perceptive Japanese Christian leader, is a contribution to the developing ecumenical Christian conversation through which we are seeking to understand what is happening in our time.

In its detailed focus on Japan, moreover, it reflects a growing recognition of the need for specifics. Our ecumenical conversation has in large part produced sweeping surveys and broad interpretations, both social and theological, and these have been of great value in orienting us to the broad outlines of the new period we have entered. But they are not enough in themselves, for we do not meet history in the gross but in the concrete. It has a fleshly particularity to it that cannot quite be fitted into generalizations, as any close examination of the different countries of Asia would reveal.

This is certainly true of Japan, which has in many ways passed through the revolution (or at least its opening stages) toward which much of Southeast Asia presses. The colonialism against which the latter countries have fought was never fastened upon Japan in modern times. The national dignity they seek has, save for a few short years, long been a prized possession in Japan. The technology and industrialization to which they look for the overcoming of poverty has been the basis of the Japanese economy for some time and has lifted her standing of living above that of the rest of Asia.

Yet it is also clear that these gains have hardly brought for her a brave new world of unmixed hope and blessing. As the first major Asian power in modern times, Japan has known the temptations toward aggrandizement that go with national power. No other powerful nation has proved immune to these temptations, and the new nations of Southeast Asia will be as sorely tempted as they grow in strength. Moreover, the impact of industrialization upon Japanese life has compounded old problems and brought new ones—in the vast spiritual and social dislocations that have come with great urban concentrations of rootless laboring people, the loosening fabric of family life, the deadening factory work, and so on. In this respect, many of Japan's problems are closely akin to those of the West, and they are serious problems that the newer nations of Asia have yet to encounter in their full dimensions.

It is one of the great values of Dr. Takenaka's presentation that he has made these and other problems clear in his brief but comprehensive survey of the Christian movement in Japan in its double dialogue with God and the culture in which it lives. As he traces the church's grappling with the many facets of that culture—its work at feudal reform, its influence in the birth of labor unions and the bettering of working conditions, its response to the social problems thrown up by industrialization, its wrestling with the problem of nationalism, its contributions to education, social welfare, and so forth—he offers, in a form not otherwise available, a detailed and documented study of great value for our understanding of the church at work in Japan.

But one further word should be said. This book can be simply a source of interesting information, or it can be an occasion for a real encounter with fellow Christians. The information is relatively unimportant; the encounter is all important. The picture Dr. Takenaka presents is one of very real people and of a very real Christian community. In their struggle with the concrete realities of life in Japan and their effort to be faithful in response to God's leading, they stand in the same place that we in our culture are (or should be) standing. Their culture is in many ways different from our own, but like ours it is a human culture in which God works to transform and make new. And in our common wrestling with what it means to respond to God's working, we have much that we can learn from each other.

It is, moreover, a picture that, like our own, is peopled with very human Christians and churches with all the limitations and intimations of strength that go with being human. It does not idealize the church nor beguile us with any illusions about a massive transformation of the life of Japan. It does offer us a real glimpse of renewals in the lives of people, of the faith that sends them forth to work, of the transformations in culture that are effected by God's working in their lives and in their common life. It recalls to us, through the medium of other people in another land, what God wills to do with us in our culture. To see this church and these people with eyes that look with them and not at them, to see their problems and responsibility as our problems and responsibility, and to make their history a part of our history

7

can be for us of value. It can, indeed, by God's grace be an event of reconciliation that gives substance to our unity in Christ and confirms the oneness of our Christian mission.

Robert Wood

CHAPTER ONE:

Protestant Beginnings

God in his redemptive love is at work in human history. And his church in every land is called to the task of reconciliation and renewal, both within a particular society or culture and—as part of the Church Universal—in the relations between nations and blocks of nations. This reconciliation and renewal are not easy. Before the radical gift of resurrected life, had to come the agony of the cross. Within our several churches we are called to a thorough-going repentance, that difficult willingness to give up the self we have been and to die in order that we may begin to live. We are called to live with the renewing power of God at work in us and through us, giving the church the courage and the wisdom to be more truly the Church. And we are called into the very midst of the world where God is at work in the social conflicts of our times, preparing men for himself as he plows up the soil of old pride and injustice of race or of class or of nation.

If the church is to heed this call, there is need for encounter between Christians of different nations and traditions because, as members of the Church Universal, we are all dependent upon and involved with one another. Where such encounter does occur, it provides a new perspective and critique both for our understanding of historic events and the discharge of political and social responsibility and for our work within our own churches. It is in the hope of furthering such understanding between Japanese and Western Christians that this study book has been undertaken.

The Christian church in Japan, along with the Japanese nation, in these postwar years is faced with momentous problems and vast opportunities. The way in which these are met will be fateful for generations to come. Japan has emerged with extreme rapidity from decaying feudalism into a modern industrialized nation; her total cultural situation is confusedly complex. The present day social and political structures have been deeply affected by the necessities that so rapid a transformation dictated, and the Christian church in Japan cannot be understood apart from this context of the precipitous birth of a nation.

The year 1868 is a dividing line in Japanese history. In that year the decaying Bakufu feudal regime was overthrown and the modernization of Japan was begun under the Meiji Restoration. The breakdown of the Bakufu feudalism was accompanied by, or set in motion, certain social forces and alliances with which the new regime had to deal and which largely limited and shaped its policies. In 1868 feudal Japan had been governed for two hundred years by the strongest of the many feudal lords, the Tokugawa Bakufu. The social structure was rigid and hierarchical. Under the Bakufu were the lesser lords, each with his domain, his warrior group (the samurai), and his peasants. The samurai received a regular stipend from his lord. In return his sword was always at his lord's service. The peasant lived at a subsistence level, having to give to the lord the majority of his crops. The Bakufu tried to make Japan economically self-sufficient. Until nearly the end of the Bakufu power, a policy of extreme isolation from other nations (Japan's famous Closed Door Policy) had been followed and violent antiforeign feeling was stirred up and encouraged.

In the last decade of the feudal period, internal unrest along with external pressures drove the Bakufu regime to

10

make trade agreements with the United States. There followed a grave economic crisis that affected all social groups. This late feudal period can be characterized by an increasingly miserable and dissatisfied peasantry; by a warrior class (the samurai) who could no longer live on what they were paid by their lords and who, because they had the least to lose in the old order, largely supplied the leadership and intelligentsia in the movement for revolt and reform; by dissatisfied merchants who needed a stable centralized government powerful enough to deal with the economic crisis; and by feudal lords long jealous of the Bakufu power. The antiforeign feeling that the Bakufu had so carefully fostered was now turned against them for having entered into relations with foreign powers. Internationally the position of Japan was very weak. It is not surprising that civil war broke out. It did not last long.

The new government, an autocratic, intelligent group of fine statesmen whom the liberal and sensitive young Emperor Meiji had gathered around himself, aimed to transform Japan from a disintegrating feudalism into an industrialized modern nation, independent and powerful. The reforms they carried out were entirely in the interests of accomplishing their aim; they were practical rather than ideological in nature. What they achieved is astonishing.

In the first ten years of the Meiji period, all taxes were centralized and the feudal lords who thus lost their revenue were compensated by the government with an allotment worth half their previous income. They were no longer required to support the samurai to whom the government also paid pensions. Later these allotments were ended by a lump sum payment, which made it possible for many of the lords and samurai to start or invest in new industrial enterprises. Also within this period, the legal inequality of the different classes was ended and the insignia and the distinctive dress of the different classes were forbidden. State support was withdrawn from Buddhism. Schools were established, conscription was introduced, and calendar and monetary reforms were carried out. New industries were started by the government, and private industry in key fields was subsidized.

In all of this, however, the traditional hierarchical system was simplified and strengthened. There was no question of introducing democratic structures. The centuries-old habit of hierarchy, the traditional system of obligation to family, superiors, and the Emperor was reinforced by the designation of particular duties to the "proper station." The speed with which the reforms were accomplished has meant that, of necessity, many of the changes have not yet been socially and culturally assimilated—even today the feudal and the industrial still exist side by side in confusing relationships.

THE FIRST DECADES

Protestantism first came to Japan in the last years of the feudal Bakufu regime and the early years of the Meiji Restoration. Thus it came, as we have seen, in the midst of far-reaching social change and at a time when the nation was in headlong transition from the feudal to the modern era. This early period had a marked influence upon the subsequent life of the church, and it is important to note the social background out of which the early Christians came and the kind of practical response that stemmed from their faith. What was the political, social, and religious context out of which people first came into the Christian faith? What motives led them in their attempts to interpret this faith to their country? What sort of theology and ethics did the first missionaries teach?

After Japan opened her door to the Western countries, Americans were assured the free exercise of their religion by the commerce treaties of 1858. They were also given the right to erect suitable buildings for worship, but the anti-Christian laws remained in force for the Japanese.

12

In front of the governor's residence, there was a notice board with a list of "forbidden things," the first of which was the "evil sect of Christianity." Large rewards were offered to informers against the hated sect. Converts were persecuted severely, many being cast into prison; and a rigid system of espionage was maintained over all suspected of sympathizing with the Christian movement.

In addition to the law, which prohibited Christianity, the general feeling of the common people was definitely aligned against Christians. For them this was a "foreign" religion, known only as the "fearful sect," that had been introduced into their country by the Jesuits and had been severely persecuted by the Bakufu government for over two hundred years. For the samurai, the feudal warrior whose role was most influential throughout this era, there were two watchwords that demanded utmost fidelity: *"Jo-i"* (Away with the foreigners), and *"Son-no"* (Honor the Emperor). Psychologically it would take more than a legal relaxation to overcome the emotional response that was brought into the mind of each samurai when he heard these words. These were the circumstances of oppression into which the Christian gospel first had to be introduced. Certainly any man or woman who accepted the faith at that time needed a special personal commitment and a decisive courage in order to be a disciple of Christ.

Nevertheless, in 1859 representatives of three American denominations arrived. At first they had to bide their time, making their preparation, learning Japanese, teaching English, translating the Bible and other Christian literature.

In December, 1871, two years before the anti-Christian laws were dropped, a group of missionaries, together with a few English-speaking residents, began a series of prayer meetings that continued into January of the following year. Into this group came a few Japanese students from the English classes—some through curiosity, others through a desire to please their teachers. But week by week the group became larger so that on March 10, 1872, the first Japanese Christian church was organized in Yokohama, made up of two previously baptized middle-aged men and nine students who were baptized on that day. Throughout the year several more students joined the church, principally under the influence of the Reverend James Ballagh. The students in this group called themselves the Yokohama Band.

This church in Yokohama was significant not only because it was the first organized Protestant church in Japan, but also because out of this group came many distinguished leaders such as Hogi Oshikawa, Kajinosuke Ibuka, Yoshiyasu Ogama, and Masahisa Uemura.

Another important aspect of this church was the refusal of its members to classify themselves denominationally. They insisted on expressing a simple evangelical faith instead of becoming involved in the complex differences of Western traditions. This spirit of ecumenicity was largely due to the influence of the early missionaries. The record of the first convention of missionaries in Yokohama in September, 1872, shows a decided resolution to keep the Japanese church free of divisiveness along denominational lines.

In 1873 the Meiji government dropped the anti-Christian edicts. That year Christians in Tokyo formed the Shinei Church. In 1874 churches were formed in Kobe and Osaka. Again the avoidance of denominational labels was stressed.

In addition to the Yokohama Band, two other groups should also be mentioned here because of their importance in providing leaders for the Protestant church in Japan. One was the group at Kumamoto; the other was that at Sapporo.

The first of these, the Kumamoto Band, as they called themselves, got a start under the leadership of Captain L. L. Janes. The feudal lord of Higo, desiring to participate in the Meiji Restoration, saw the need for establishing a school to train leaders for future government service. The best students

14

in the area were enlisted and gathered at Kumamoto to study Western science, history, languages, and culture. Captain Janes was brought in as a central person for the whole program. He taught quite a wide range of subjects himself, such as mathematics, geography, history, physics, chemistry, geology, and astronomy. For the first three years, he expressed his Christian faith only by example; then he began to speak about the necessity for understanding the Bible, and in his own home he opened a Bible study class that met every week.

One after another the students began to believe the Christian faith, and on January 30, 1876, thirty-five students climbed Mt. Hanaoka on the outskirts of the city and signed a Declaration of Belief in Christianity. Among them were such future leaders in the church as Tsuneteru Miyagawa, Danjo Ebina, Tokio Yokoi, Tsurin Kanamori, Kazutami Ukita, Kotaro Shimomura. Hiromichi Kozaki later joined the group. Many of these students went on to Doshisha University where they were profoundly influenced by Joseph Hardy Niishima and continued to be an important group within the early church of Japan.

A third band, in Sapporo, was founded under the leadership of Colonel W. S. Clark. Dr. Clark, President of Massachusetts Agricultural College at the time, took a temporary leave of absence to devote himself to the establishment of a similar institution in Sapporo in the frontier area of Hokkaido. In order to accomplish his purpose in the nine short months of his stay in Sapporo, Dr. Clark selected twenty-four students, mainly from samurai families, who had an earnest desire to serve their country through the cultivation of the Hokkaido district. He insisted that the Bible should be the basis of the morality to be taught in the new school.

Many from this group also became outstanding Christian leaders—men such as Shosuke Sato, Kazutaka Ito, Masatake Oshima, Yomonishin Kuroiwa, Inazo Nitobe, Kingo Miyabe, and Kanzo Uchimura. As we shall see later, Uchimura established the nonchurch group that has played a unique role in the relation of Christianity to society.

SAMURAI BACKGROUND

A large number of the first Christian young people in the early Meiji era were samurai (the feudal warrior class). The samurai class, along with the feudal lords and the Shinto priests, had had an extremely privileged position in the old feudal society. But under the Meiji Restoration they found themselves in a disturbing and difficult situation. The new government relieved the feudal lords of their obligation for the support of the samurai, thus plunging them into dire economic distress. Except for the comparatively few who could be taken into the new Japanese Army or Navy, this whole class now found itself without status or profession, thrust out of their old place in the social scheme. They were no longer necessary to their society in the old way. The majority of the samurai were thus faced with the necessity of a radical readjustment to the new situation. They had to seek new ways to gain a livelihood, but also they were forced to find a new meaning for their existence in the emerging national community.

Many of these young samurai turned to Occidental culture and came to missionaries with great eagerness to learn new ways of serving their nation. For many of them their loyalty was transferred from the feudal lords to the Christian Lord, whom they determined to serve even at the cost of their lives. They found new hope and new life in Christ. They believed that in Christ they had found the best way to participate in the formation of a new Japan.

One of these young people was Shimeta Niishima, who later became famous as Joseph Hardy Niishima, the founder of Doshisha University. At the time of the Restoration, he had gotten himself smuggled out of Japan to America, and while in the United States he wrote: "Unworthy as I am, I seek earnestly to serve our country. But now being away from home and transgressing bondage (breaking the national law prohibiting Japanese to leave the country), I become a disciple of God. Therefore, I hate to return again to my clan and to be satisfied with a little annuity. As I am a subject of God as well as a samurai of Japan, I believe it is my urgent task to commit myself entirely to the service of the true God in Japan."[1]

Here one can see from the beginning the root of the connection between Japanese Protestant Christianity and nationalism. The majority of early Japanese Protestants came from the socially dislocated samurai class. They found in Christ the answer to their deepest searching, but their interpretation of Christianity was inextricably shot through with their anguished search for a new sense of identity within the national community.

CONFUCIAN TRAINING

Another important fact about these early Christians is that they were intellectuals. They had been trained from youth in the Chinese classics and Confucianism. And it was Confucianism that laid the groundwork for their religious background before coming to the Christian faith. For them the moral teachings of Confucius, particularly in the school of Wang Yang Ming, (or the Jitsugaku school) provided the preparation for their acceptance of Christian ethics. In contrast to the relatively conservative and literal schools, this school emphasized the more positive spirit found in Confucian teachings. And it included a certain religious reverence toward heaven. Danjo Ebina, a member of the Kumamoto Band who had been trained in Confucianism in his boyhood, wrote:

"What made me overcome the obstacle in entering into the

[1] See page 94 for Footnotes.

17

Christian faith was that I had an insight from the Jitsugaku school, which had a positive teaching. The Shushi school had taught that one must obey one's parents with tears if they do not listen after one has admonished them three times. On the contrary, the Jitsugaku school discussed the matter of heaven and the world in relation to one's conscience; that is, one can go on his way toward heaven and in the world in spite of the rejection of parents. In the Jitsugaku school we personalized 'Heaven,' calling it *'Jyotei'* (Heavenly Emperor), believing that he saw our souls and protected us. That's when we seemed to know Christianity; we believed that *Jyotei* in Confucianism and God in Christianity are the same thing."[2] For Ebina and others this connection between the two religions was not necessarily a synthesis nor an amalgamation of the two but rather the belief that Christian revelation came as the fulfillment of Confucian preparation.

Hiromichi Kozaki expresses the same idea in his own experiences: "Though my early absorption in Confucianism might seem (to some) an obstacle to faith, it was in reality a great help. For Paul and other Jews, the religion of the Old Testament was an elementary education, a preparation for their belief in Christ; for me, this preparation was Confucianism. Paul was never ashamed that he had formerly been a most zealous believer in Judaism, but was proud of it. . . . Also Jesus says, 'Think not that I came to destroy the law and the prophets; I came not to destroy but to fulfill.' . . . We embraced Christianity because we have believed that it fulfills the spirit and the real import of Confucianism."[3]

Many of the other early Christian leaders held much the same point of view, and one can understand why they were eager to stress a continuity between their new found faith and established Japanese religious teaching. Destructive or negative attitudes on the part of Christians toward the old existing religions in the East make it very difficult for people to enter into the Christian faith. But more important than

18

this, Christianity was regarded by most Japanese as a foreign evil, and it was felt that those Japanese who did become Christian were subversive and sullied the purity of the Japanese cultural heritage. The samurai who, because of their social dislocation in this period, were the most open to Christianity were, because of this same uprooting, driven by the need to reaffirm both their involvement as samurai in the Japanese cultural tradition and their loyalty as Christians to the Japanese ethos.

These pressures resulted in a stress by the early Japanese Protestant leaders on the continuity between the Christian faith and certain forms of Japanese religious life. Thus the early church in Japan tended to be absorbed in practical work and in discovering positive relationships to the national cultural life; it developed little theological or spiritual basis for a prophetic protest against fundamental patterns or forces in that cultural life. The early leaders were concerned to show that Christianity was not "un-Japanese" (as American churches are often concerned not to seem "un-American"), and it was difficult at the same time to make the emotional reversal that would be required in order to speak out against those aspects of Japanese life that were "un-Christian."

These were formative years in the church in Japan, and this problem remains with the church today. In many Western countries Christians show this same tendency to assume a continuity between their cultural values and the Christian faith, but in Japan the reverential, religious character of the common attitude toward the Japanese nation itself brings to the problem a special dimension and intensity, not unlike that which bedeviled the church in Nazi Germany. A religious or quasi-religious attitude toward the entity of the nation, combined with a church that seeks to stress her identity with the nation, makes it nearly impossible for the church to speak to the nation with any truly prophetic word. Thus the particular pressures in the modern Japanese historical situation have

19

provided certain limitations as well as possibilities. This is the difficult framework within which the church has had to work.

EMPHASIS ON MORALITY

A strong influence in early Protestantism in Japan was a religious moralism that characterized much late nineteenth and early twentieth century Protestantism in America and was brought by the missionaries to Japan. It was a humanistic Puritanism, an ethic that had lost its theological foundation and reference. Personal discipline and morality were greatly stressed as of central importance in the Christian life. This early emphasis has been a decisive influence in the subsequent life of the church.

In Kumamoto, Captain Janes guided the students with a strict discipline and diligence. Kozaki testified to this in describing the life of the school: "In the dormitory, in accordance with the pattern of military schools, the times for going to bed and getting up, the times for meals, etc., were rigidly observed. At 10 P.M. came roll call and immediately after with not one moment of leeway allowed us, lights must go out. In the morning the rising bell was rung, and if anyone rose before that he was compelled to return to bed. After breakfast we went out into the courtyard to practice deep breathing, after which we assumed rank and file for military drill. Drinking and smoking were strictly forbidden. 'Gate-closing' was punctually observed and it was not easy to leave the grounds."[4]

In such circumstances, industry became identified with righteousness and idleness with sin. For the samurai students who were used to being brought up under the strictest of disciplines, all of this was pursued passionately.

In Sapporo, Dr. Clark felt it was necessary to teach the dignity of work among his students. According to feudal custom, students regarded labor with contempt and looked down on money as something ignoble. In order to make his students understand the holiness of labor and how it is perfectly legitimate to receive for it certain rewards without shame, Dr. Clark paid five sen per hour for agricultural field work, each student being required to work six hours per week. Right from the opening ceremony of the school, Dr. Clark demanded rigid discipine from each student in taking care of his health, in controlling his appetite, in strengthening the power of continence, and in maintaining the habit of obedience and diligence. Further, by means of a written oath, he outlawed all smoking and drinking.

In the Yokohama Band, too, the influence of American moralism was evident. One of its outstanding members later wrote in this way as he looked back to his early years: "It looked to us as if Christianity was identified with three things: expulsion of false images, prohibition of smoking and drinking, and the exaltation of monogamy."[5]

PERSISTENT PERSECUTION

In the meantime, it is important to keep in mind the difficulties in the early years of becoming a Christian at all. The early Christians in Japan faced bitter persecution and suspicion from their own countrymen, and it required a deep personal commitment and great courage in order to stand firm in their new faith. Two hundred years earlier the Roman Catholics had for a time been allowed to do missionary work in Japan, but this had been followed by terrible and persistent persecution. Thousands were put to death, many by crucifixion. Severe persecution of a less violent sort continued even after Christianity was legalized in the Meiji era.

Shortly after the Declaration of Belief in Christianity in 1876, the members of the Kumamoto Band faced serious difficulties, and the stories of the strength of their faith and courage are noteworthy. Tokio Yokoi, for instance, encountered much opposition. His father, Shonan Yokoi, had been assassinated in 1869 under suspicion of sympathy with Chris-

21

tianity, and the young Yokoi had been brought up in a family of Confucian scholars.

Every attempt was made to wipe away the influences of the father upon the son, and Yokoi was absolutely forbidden to associate in any way with Christians. Nevertheless, he resolved to become a Christian. He was imprisoned in his room, and finally his mother issued the ultimatum that unless he would renounce the Christian faith she would commit suicide. The young boy was faced with the alternative of giving up his faith or causing the death of his mother. After some attempt to postpone the crisis in the family, a conference was called with all the relatives. A compromise solution was reached whereby Tokio was allowed to go to Tokyo with the understanding that he might become a Christian but must never become a clergyman. Interestingly enough, however, at a later date Tokio did become a minister and even baptized his mother into the Imaharu Church.

Summarizing then, early Japanese Protestants came out of a samurai origin at a transitional time during the Meiji Restoration. Early Japanese Protestantism was characterized by a devotion to the service of the nation as well as loyalty to Christ; it appealed to the educated; it brought together Western learning and combined it with a Confucian preparation; and it had at its heart a religious moralism that was most compatible with the ethical emphasis of the samurai-Confucian background of the majority of its members. In this latter emphasis, it combined the virtues of discipline, hard work, and a pure life with the patience to withstand hardships and persecutions.

CHAPTER TWO:

The Christian Contribution
in the Transition from Feudalism

As we have noted, Protestantism came to Japan in the midst of the breakup of feudal society and the transition to the modern era. In this period many men and women came into the Christian faith, hoping that through it they might serve their country in the process of modernization. Despite suspicion and the dangers of persecution, these men and women made courageous efforts to follow Christ and to serve the needs of their neighbors in various fields.

The large majority of the early Japanese Christians saw that conversion is nothing less than a changing of one's whole attitude in response to the call of God. It was a general pattern that these early Christians, immediately after accepting the Christian faith, sought to express their experience through a new relation to their neighbors. They poured their energies into such fields as education, social work, the temperance movement, civil liberties, and prison reform. Many of these early Christians became the pioneers in higher education and in social work in Japan. With sincere religious motivation and advanced skills and training, the Christian churches made a great contribution to Japan in the process of social reform.

The churches made steady progress in their expansion throughout the nineteenth century. By 1900 the total membership was 37,068, distributed in 416 local churches. In terms of quantity, of course, this was still a very small minority, less than one-tenth of one per cent of the total population. Yet, qualitatively, the Christians were a creative group, participating significantly in social reform.

THE CHRISTIAN CONTRIBUTION TO EDUCATION

Most of the Christian missions started their work in Japan with the establishment of educational institutions. By 1889 eight colleges for men and twenty-eight higher schools for women had been founded by Christians. Most of the outstanding Christian schools that still exist today were founded in these early years of Protestantism, and they have maintained their influence in spite of difficulties and opposition.

Three particularly significant contributions in education were made by Christians during this early period: (1) Christians first introduced into Japan the pattern of the modern Western university; (2) Christians stressed education for women and introduced coeducation; (3) Christian education in Japan maintained a unique character in its stress on the development of personality and the worth of the individual.

In regard to the first of these, during the feudalistic era there had been no institution to be compared with the modern university. Most education was Confucian and centered around the private relationship of teacher to student.

When in 1873 the anti-Christian edicts were removed, the missions started to develop their English classes into Christian institutions of higher education. For example, Talcott and Duddley's school developed into Kobe College and Davis' school became Doshisha University. It is significant to note that Doshisha University was established two years before Tokyo University, which is the oldest and largest government university.

Secondly, in regard to coeducation and the education of women, it was also the Christians who took the lead. One of the first instances of coeducation occurred in Kumamoto in the school established by Captain Janes. Mrs. Janes had been teaching two girls separately, and, when the time came for her child to be born, Captain Janes combined her class with his own. For the boys such a move was completely unbelievable. Under the Confucian system there was a rule that boys and girls were to be separated in all public meetings after the age of seven years. The boys felt that coeducation was a compromise of their traditional feudal superiority and privilege, and they made a protest to Captain Janes.

Their representative, Danjo Ebina, went to the teacher with the reasons why it would be impossible to mix girls and boys in the same school. Janes, however, knew that Ebina had a very deep personal respect for his own mother and so after listening patiently to the young man's purpose, he simply asked the question, "Is your mother a man or a woman?" This, of course, left the student tongue-tied, and from there Janes went on to explain to him and to the other students the importance of the role of the woman in the family and in society. He encouraged them to recognize the need for adequate education for women as well as men. An interesting footnote to this incident lies in the fact that of these two girls who were the pioneers of coeducation in Japan, Hatsuko Tokutomi later became Mrs. Jiro Yuasa, mother of Hachiro Yuasa, President of International Christian University, and the other, Miyako Yokoi, later married Danjo Ebina—the very same brilliant young student who objected so heartily to the inclusion of these girls in his class.

The next twenty years showed a rapid advance in education for women through the establishment of Christian schools. Forty-four Christian girls' high schools were organized before 1899, about 70 per cent of the number of Christian girls' high schools in Japan today.

The third significant contribution that the Christian schools made was their emphasis upon the development of personality and the worth of the individual. Government schools were carried on under formal and strict regulations for teaching, whereas the Christian schools encouraged the development of informal and intimate relationships between teacher and student. Christians tried to demonstrate their belief in the worth of the individual and to clarify the meaning of personality through education. The Christian pioneering effort in women's education brought a wider understanding of the right of women to education, a right that had been denied them in feudalistic society. Education in the mission schools, particularly in the girls' schools, while being puritanical was not feudalistic nor reactionary as was the case in the government girls' schools. Thus it is not surprising that the leaders in the Women's Liberation Movement were mainly alumnae of the mission schools.

Despite the significant contributions and pioneering advances that have been mentioned above, Christian educational institutions in Japan through the years have had to face many problems and difficulties both from within and from without. One of these problems came in the strong upsurge of nationalism in Japan that partly accompanied and partly became a reaction to the introduction of Western culture. The Constitution of 1889 and the Imperial Rescript on Education in 1890 both heightened the trend toward nationalism. The Sino-Japanese War of 1894-95 and the Russo-Japanese War of 1904-05 further helped to unify and intensify this nationalistic fervor.

Christian schools, which had sprung up quickly without reference to any foundation in Japanese culture, faced a serious crisis. Some seventeen Christian schools had to close their doors during this period because of decreases in enrollment, and there was also a sharp decline in the number of students in the theological schools. Other Christian schools that had expanded their capacities and equipment found it very difficult to continue in the face of decreasing enrollment. Many Christian schools that had been financially independent were unable to continue such a policy and had to secure support from western European and American mission boards. This was a difficult compromise for many Japanese Christian leaders.

For a period after 1897, the government prohibited all religious instruction, even in Christian schools. Also the students in Christian schools were not exempted from military service until graduation as were students in the government schools.

Another problem for the missionary school came in the rapid advance in the level of education in the government schools. Although the Christian schools had been pioneers in higher education, with the government's rapid introduction of Western learning and strong financial support of education, the government schools were soon raised to superior academic standards. Even to this day the Christian schools have great difficulty in maintaining as high academic qualifications for their teaching staffs as the government schools. The missionary teachers have always had language limitations. Lack of financial support has often made it difficult for the Christian universities to obtain the best in the way of Japanese professors. Furthermore, the emphasis upon developing moral virtue and in maintaining spiritual and devotional life has meant that the Christian schools have generally neglected certain of the academic disciplines. For example, very few Christian universities have developed departments of natural science.

These problems of the Christian university tend to persist in Japan even to this time. Without receiving government assistance, the Christian schools feel forced to take a large enrollment in order to meet the high expenses. The resulting high ratio of students to teachers only makes more difficult the problem of developing a person in his wholeness and of educating the student in a Christian community with a proper balance and relationship between faith and reason.

In the field of social work, the pioneering nature of the Christian contribution has been highly significant, and, even more than in the case of education, this contribution in social work continues to this day. In the fall of 1956, the Japanese government was asked to name the four most outstanding leaders in the field of social work in Japanese history. The four then nominated were: Juji Ishii, founder of the Okayama Orphanage—the largest orphanage in that district; Kosuke Tomeoka, who worked in prison reform and established a reformatory; Gumpei Yamamuro, founder of the Salvation Army and social settlements and a leader in the temperance movement; and Takeo Iwahashi, the founder of the Light House in Osaka, a center for those who like himself are blind. Christians—all of them!

Another incident to show the leadership of Christians in social work came in 1926 when the government made awards to those who had contributed most to the development of social work since the Meiji era. Twenty-two out of thirty-two people receiving these awards were Christian.

One of the first of these many Christian social workers was Taneaki Hara, who started work among released criminals in Kobe in 1884. He also worked with and for prisoners, giving himself to be the prison chaplain in Kobe. In 1884 he was jailed because he published pictures of those who had been sent to prison for their participation in the civil liberty movement. The care of prisoners and ex-prisoners has continued through the years to be a strong focus for Christian concern.

The temperance movement, after its introduction to Japan by early missionaries, made great progress through the efforts of Japanese Christians. As a result of the efforts of Mrs. Mary Clemmer Leavitt, who came from the United States, many temperance associations were formed throughout the country. In 1886, under the direction of Kaji Yajima, the Tokyo Temperance Association was organized with fifty-six members.

Within a year its membership was more than one hundred.

Christians have also worked devotedly toward the liberation of women in Japan. In Gumma Prefecture, as early as 1882, a strong movement arose under Christian initiative to work against prostitution. Other Christian efforts, aimed toward the extension of civil rights to women, came to fruition after World War II when women, for the first time, were given the right to vote in national elections. At that time thirty-nine women were elected to the House of Representatives. In this field of women's suffrage, the Japan Women's Temperance Association has been active since 1920, at which time the association officially created a department on legislation and helped to organize the associated body called the Association for Women's Suffrage. Another fruit of the endeavors of these groups came in the enactment of the Anti-Prostitution Act in 1956. Although the law does not solve the whole problem (in some ways it has created new problems), it is significant that this is the first law in the history of Japan that bans prostitution.

In another area, missionaries contributed much with the introduction of Western medicine. At first missionary doctors like Dr. Hepburn and Dr. Berry practiced medicine in their homes or in government dispensaries. But soon they established new hospitals in the major cities of Japan. For instance, in 1902, with support from the Protestant Episcopal Church, St. Luke's Hospital—later called St. Luke's International Medical Center in Tokyo—was established. It has become one of the most outstanding medical centers in Japan.

Another fine example of Christian medical work was Hakuai Kai in Okayama. This work was initiated in 1891 through the efforts of Alice P. Adams, a missionary of the American Board, and it still stands as one of the oldest and finest social settlements in Japan. It provides a free nursery, education for working girls, and a medical hospital in the midst of the crowded homes of that city.

29

Significant medical work was also done by Christian missionaries and Japanese Christians in the field of leprosy and tuberculosis. Previously those who had contracted these diseases were ostracized and left to themselves without care or fellowship of any kind. Hana Riddel of the Protestant Episcopal Mission started a leper hospital in Kumamoto in 1895, and a similar institution was built by a Miss Youngman in Tokyo in 1895. The St. Barnabas Mission was another unique attempt made by Christians in Gumma Prefecture. A separate community for lepers was established here near a hot spring. All of these separate pieces of work with lepers have been appreciated greatly by the Japanese government.

In 1927 the Christian social workers in various fields throughout the country gathered to form the Association for Christian Social Work in Japan. This association began by noting the significant contributions that Christians have made through the years in the various fields of education and social work. It noted especially that the work has usually been in pioneering areas, providing a remarkable demonstration of love in combination with advanced training and resources.

Despite the glories of the past, Christian social workers in Japan realize that they are facing a new era. In the course of its program for modernization, the government started public social work agencies. With the vast resources of the government brought to bear in their field, the government agencies began (as was the case in education) to dwarf the efforts of the Christian groups and to make their work seem relatively unimportant. At this point perhaps the most significant contribution that can be made by the Christian social work agencies lies in the continuing challenge that the Christian understanding of man holds out to the developing social work methods and techniques, which tend to be manipulative in character and to usurp to themselves a disproportionate importance. Advanced methods should be utilized by all means, and new techniques must constantly be acquired. Technology, however, is not the end, only the means to the end, and the Christian in social work stands within a unique perspective from which to bring a corrective.

At this point in Japanese history, it may very well be that the significant efforts in Christian social reform in Japan are in the field of organized social action. In the past it has been a great adventure for small groups of Christians to support various social work projects. But this has generally been done in a spirit of charity that has expressed both paternalistic and individualistic sentiments. Despite the external growth of churches in recent years, these same churches have become less critical toward the causes of existing social evils, thus widening the gap separating them from the lower classes except for such contacts as are made through charity programs. The emphasis on social work tended to overshadow the approach of social action, which should seek to deal with the causes of social evil rather than simply with the results. The social concern of the Protestant churches was expressed in efforts to secure decent living for all people as a charity rather than as a right of the people.

Since World War II the Japanese government has moved in the direction of establishing a welfare state and is attempting to develop a social welfare program. However, the program is still in its initial stages, limited by a low budget and a relatively small number of people who participate in the program. Certainly among the crucial tasks of the Christian church in Japan today are to insist upon the irrevocable value of all persons based on God's love for them made manifest in Christ and to call the government to an awareness of its social responsibility for all in the community.

RURAL REFORM

The rural area in Japan is still predominantly feudal. Despite the process of industrialization, a large proportion of the population remains in the field of agriculture, amounting to 45.4 per cent, or around 37,800,000 people. Among these rural people, traditional feudalistic social patterns and attitudes still have a tenacious hold. This feudal outlook is seen in the rural communities in oppression of women, the special privilege of the eldest son, community pressure upon the stranger, conservative attitudes toward progressive opinions, authoritarian and hierarchical patterns of life, and family domination over individual freedom.

In these areas also the traditional religions, such as Shintoism and Buddhism, are inseparable from life as a whole and help to maintain the conservative climate. Shintoism, which originally was animistic, later developed a nationalistic strain and became the main ideological force in imperial Japan. Buddhism, on the other hand, with its other-worldly concern has turned to the life of contemplation, looking for deliverance in the future from bondage in this life. Religious belief in Buddhism and Shintoism were held simultaneously. Worship at the Shinto shrines, centering in religious devotion to the Emperor, related the individual to the mystical entity of the nation. Buddhist religious rites tended to reinforce the relation of the individual to the family through ancestor worship and the burial of the dead.

In the face of these conservative tendencies, it has been natural for Christianity to encounter opposition and difficulties when it entered the rural community. In 1884 the church in Takahashi in Okayama was stoned by a crowd. Its windows were broken, and its fence and gate were thrown into the river. In the period of rapid Westernization, Christianity was accepted somewhat in rural areas, but it was caught soon afterward in the upsurge of antiforeign feeling. Today in Japan 60 per cent of the Protestant churches are located in the cities; 230 out of 270 cities in Japan have churches. On the other hand, 70 per cent of the towns and 97 per cent of the villages have no churches at all.

This, however, does not mean that the churches have not

32

been patiently trying to establish themselves in the rural community. There have been several notable instances of success, particularly where individual Christians have organized new patterns of communal life based on the Christian gospel—for example, at Omihachiman in Shiga Prefecture, in the Immanuel Village in Hokkaido, and in the Annaka Village in Gumma Prefecture. Since World War II there have been renewed efforts to extend the church into the rural areas.

After World War II the land reform policy that was carried out by the American Occupation from 1946-50 brought great changes to rural society generally. Before the war 70 per cent of the Japanese farmers rented all or part of their land and of these one third owned no land at all. Now, after the land reform, 70 per cent of the farmers own all of their land, only 6 per cent are tenants, and the remaining 24 per cent own some land. For the most part, the land reform has been carried out in a peaceful and relatively satisfactory way. The director for the land reform, Laurence Hewes, summarized its effect on the old landlord and tenant by saying that two great feudal classes had been abolished and that, for the first time, peasants have the full stature of free men.

This reform, however, is just the beginning. The same kind of process must be worked out for forest land as well as for farm land. The church must see to it that such changes, or a more just distribution of land, should have a counterpart in more just relations between persons. Unless the deep meaning of the dignity of man and a real sense of community can be established in the grass roots of rural life, the change that has taken place might become merely external and enforced rather than internal and a genuine change in rural life. The Christian gospel, which proclaims the redeeming love of God and restores the real sense of communal life, has an immeasurable role to play in the reconstruction of the rural community in Japan.

CHAPTER THREE:

The Christian Influence
in the Developing Industrial Society

Japan under the Meiji Restoration embarked upon a course of rapid industrialization. In meeting the challenges and needs created by the growth of an industrial society, some of the Christian leaders took an active part in the movement for social reform. They pioneered in such areas as the establishment of labor unions, the organization of the farmer's union, and the co-operative movement.

One of those who provided an impetus in this direction, turning the attention of Christians to the need for social reform in the developing industrial society, was D. W. Learned. He taught politics and economics from a liberal Christian point of view for fifteen years at Doshisha University. His lectures were published in 1887 and in 1891, thus providing for the spread of his influence throughout the country. In these lectures Learned analyzed capitalism and pointed out the economic and social deficiencies in the system. His influence along with that of other missionaries led to an emphasis on social problems at Doshisha. From among the Doshisha students of this period came some of the great leaders of the socialist movement, such men as Isoo Abe and Tomoyoshi Murai as well as such pioneers in social work as Gumpei Yamamuro and Kosuke Tomeoka.

One of the earliest introductions to socialist thinking was

made by Hiromichi Kozaki, one of the leaders in the Protestant church at that time. His article in the Christian periodi-
cal, *Rikugo Zasshi,* in April, 1881, introduced the economic
theories of Lassalle, Marx, Engels, and Bakunin. These contributions, however, were mainly in the nature of a theoretical introduction and exhortations to socialism rather than
actual participation in the socialist movement, which did not
start until the last decade of the nineteenth century.

The particular problems and dilemmas of the developing
labor and socialist movements in Japan were produced by
three main factors working together in the political and social
situation. These factors were (1) the unstable character of the
labor force, (2) the alliance of Japanese industry with government, and (3) the government repression of all liberal
movements.

During the Meiji era there was a wide increase in the hold-
ings of the noncultivating landowners and a corresponding
increase in the number of tenant farmers. Excessively high
rents for the tenants, limited income, and a growing population meant that most of the Japanese farmers were forced to
find additional sources of income in order to stay alive. With
the rise of a modern factory industry, more and more of the
tenant farmers or members of their families, particularly the
women, left the countryside for the city to supplement their
meager family incomes. The rural areas thus became the
great source of cheap labor employed in the industries in
Japan. However, those workers who came out of the villages
did not provide a stable labor force, for they went to the city
only for short periods, returning to the village at times of unemployment, for marriage, or to help with the harvest. The
constantly shifting nature of the labor force has made it extremely difficult to undertake long-range education programs
for labor and to develop leadership out of the ranks of labor.

In the interests of a rapid movement toward industrialization, the Meiji regime had itself started industries, and it re-

35

tained the direction and control over those that were related to the building up of the Army and Navy. But the government had also borrowed heavily from the great Japanese financial houses in order to carry out its program for the modernization of Japan. Thus there was a close interrelation between industry and government with little chance of government pressure on industry on behalf of labor.

In fact, the government exerted strong repressive pressure upon liberal movements in general and the labor movement in particular. The Peace Preservation Law of 1887 radically restricted the liberal movements, and the Peace Police Law of 1889 condemned to imprisonment and hard labor any person who tried to organize a union.

Such government repression of labor organizations as something subversive made almost impossible any widespread labor education or a long-term program of action. It also tended to limit the leadership of the labor movement to radicals and professionals who used the workers occasionally, only as a means for creating agitation. Furthermore, the situation resulted in a wide cleavage between the leaders of the labor movement and the workers. In general, the strategy of the leadership was to achieve sudden victory through violence rather than a strategy of gradual reform within the framework of the existing order.

THE EARLY CHRISTIAN SOCIALIST MOVEMENT

Despite the above mentioned difficulties, after the Sino-Japanese War of 1894-95, there was rapid development of thinking in support of a labor movement in Japan. It is widely recognized that the early labor and socialist movements were notably influenced by Western culture in general and Christian ethics in particular. Two streams are clearly discernible in the early socialist movement in Japan—one was developed out of dialectic materialism, the other built upon the Christian faith. The socialist movement developed through

36

the interaction of these two groups, which sometimes co-operated and at other times were antagonistic to each other.

It was an epoch-making event when on June 25, 1897, at the Tokyo Y.M.C.A., the Association for the Formation of Labor Unions was born. In its statement of purpose this organization resolved "to maintain the rights of labor, to sustain the good tradition, to remove abuses, and to encourage the formation of unions which will unite labor." In 1898 this organization had over 1,000 members; a year later the membership had reached 5,700. Many Christians were active in the formation of this union; Sen Katayama was appointed staff secretary and a member of the publication and lecture committee; Sumio Shimada, Tomoyoshi Murai, and Isoo Abe acted as councilors. Although the organization made no explicit mention of Christianity, it implicitly accepted Christian principles. The leaders called for mutual support among laboring people and, in the interest of labor's welfare, advocated gradual and peaceful means of reform rather than sudden and violent revolution. The practical principles by which Katayama and others led the labor union movement were expressed by a statement appearing in the first issue of *The Labor World,* a monthly magazine that Katayama began in 1897. In this he said, "The policy of *The Labor World* is to manifest two mottoes: 'Labor Is Holy' and 'Union Is Power.'"

Under the leadership of the association, several unions were organized. One of these, the Iron Workers' Union, was the first labor union in the modern sense in Japan. It had 1,075 members in eleven factories when it was organized in 1897. Another union formed under the guidance of the association the following year was the Association for Reform, an organization of railroad engineers and firemen of the Japan Railway Company. Shortly after the formation of this union, the railway engineers and firemen went on strike to protest the discharge of ten persons because of their demand for higher wages. This strike ended in a victory for the labor union and a clear demonstration of organized labor's power.

The other union that was organized at this time was the Printing Workers' Union, established in 1898. The president of the union was Saburo Shimada, a Christian, a member of the Association for the Formation of Labor Unions, a champion of the temperance movement, and a crusader against licensed prostitution.

Thus in this period Christians in the labor movement, mainly through the Association for the Formation of Labor Unions, made an effort to advance the dignity of work, emphasized the necessity of mutual assistance, and helped in the organization of unions.

In addition to the practical efforts toward organizing labor unions and educating labor regarding the need for mutual assistance, there was also an urgent need for a systematic study of social problems, and in 1890 the Association for the Study of Social Problems was formed by Yujiro Miyake, Sen Katayama, Teiichi Sukuma, Tokichi Tarui, and Charles E. Garst. There were about two hundred members including people of different points of view.

Out of this group, in the fall of 1898, came the Association for the Study of Socialism, which was concerned to understand the principles of socialism and their application to Japanese society. The members met regularly at the hall of the Unitarian Society in Tokyo for lectures and discussions. Although this association also had members from various backgrounds, Christian humanists constituted its main body. Eight of the fourteen original members were associated with the Unitarian Society of Tokyo. Many from this group went to America for study and were greatly influenced there both by liberal theology and by socialism. One of the non-Christian socialists who joined in this group commented upon the Christians in the group as follows: "This association was established mainly by Christians. Although these people went to the Western countries to study Christianity, they knew at the same time the material circumstances of actual society and could not limit their studies entirely to abstract theology. Rather they sought to apply a Christian spirit to the material world."[1]

In 1900, when Isoo Abe became the chairman of the association, the nonsocialist members withdrew, and the name was changed to the Socialist Association, reflecting a readiness to participate in an actual movement. In addition to convictions arrived at through theoretical study, other factors were influencing the members of the association to give serious consideration to the socialist creed. The constant oppression of the labor movement by the government was sharply intensified by the enactment of a new Peace Preservation Law in 1900. This law again put heavy restrictions upon the labor movement, and Katayama as a practical leader of the union movement expressed his criticism in *The Labor World*: "A strike is the means whereby labor may make its final bargain under the constitution. This is the right of labor, and if one makes an effort for this purpose, he should be permitted freedom of speech and not be suppressed by police as long as he does not threaten the life of employers nor the destruction of their property."[2] The repressive measures of the government continued, and Katayama became an advocate of socialism.

As the tension against the labor movement grew, there was a decided swing toward a more radical approach by the labor movement. After the Sino-Japanese War there was a wave of sit-downs, strikes, and unemployment that created a still wider economic cleavage between management and labor.

Also, while the government maintained its oppression by laws against the labor movement, there were no laws such as factory laws, employer's liability, or working men's insurance laws to guard the rights of working people. Many women and children were mercilessly employed in the factories. One document illustrates how severe was the condition for young girls temporarily employed in the cotton mills:

"Everyday working hours were never less than thirteen or fourteen hours or in some cases they even went as high as seventeen to eighteen hours. . . . The night shift involved such hard work that very few were willing to accept it; therefore, the company ordered girls who were staying in the company dormitory to go back to work after their regular day and to continue on into the next morning. In one case a girl worked for thirty-six hours without any sleep, and similar practices were not rare."[3]

In view of the situation, those who were concerned with social reform came to realize the limitations of a fraternal unionism that aimed at the development of harmony between labor and management. They realized that political action was necessary in order to bring about a socialism that would benefit the working people and advance their total welfare. Thus, in 1901, a group of socialists who had been studying together in the association formed the Social Democratic Party. Those who founded the party were Katayama, Abe, Kinoshita, Kawakami, Nishikawa, and Kotoku, all of whom were Christians with the exception of Kotoku, who was influenced by materialistic socialism. However, again difficulty was encountered, for when they applied to the authorities for permission to promote such a party, the party was dissolved by the Minister of Home Affairs.

This party, the first of socialist parties in Japan, was not radical nor did it aim at violent methods. It was dedicated to a thoroughgoing and gradual reform of society. The declaration of the party reflected a general implicit belief in Christian humanism among its leaders. They expressed sympathy with the oppressed workers; they protested against the domination of the privileged classes; and they contended against the wide cleavage between the poor and the rich. Its spirit was one of pacifism rather than violent conflict, of gradual progressivism rather than revolution, and of lawful means rather than a disrespect for the existing laws. The positive goals laid down in the party platform expressed the ideals of democratic socialism. In its first platform the party laid out eight points that were considered to be "ideal": (1) universal brotherhood; (2) abolition of the Army and Navy and the realization of international peace; (3) abolition of class distinctions, and political and economic equality; (4) common ownership of land and capital; (5) public ownership of railways, steamships, canals, bridges, and other means of communication; (6) equitable distribution of wealth; (7) equal share of political rights by all people; and (8) complete education of all at the expense of the government.

Despite the fact that the party was dissolved by the Minister of Home Affairs, the Socialist Association continued to work on education and propaganda for socialism. In the fall of 1903, they organized the Commoner's Association, and they started a weekly journal called *Commoner's News,* which advocated socialism and took a pacifist stand against the Russo-Japanese War of 1904-05. Pressure from the government continued, however, and the Socialist Association was ordered to dissolve on November 16, 1904. In addition to government pressure, the Commoner's Association also was having problems of its own. It was having financial difficulties, and serious divisions were arising from the ideological differences between the Christian socialists and the materialistic Marxist socialists. As the external pressure became stronger, the internal difficulties increased, and the Commoner's Association finally dissolved in 1905.

After the dissolution of the Commoner's Association, the socialist camp was divided in several directions. Christian socialists like Abe, Ishikawa, and Kinoshita gathered together to publish their journal, *The New Era.* The materialistic or atheistic socialists like Yamaguchi and Nishikawa established *The Light* as their organ. Sakai started the independent magazine called *The Home Magazine.* These men not only separated but also bitterly criticized one another. This existence of deep antagonism among the top level intellectual leaders and their isolation from the working class were unfortunate things in the history of the Japanese labor movement.

In summary, we recognize the pioneering efforts toward industrial reform that were made by Christians. The socialist movement was initiated mainly by a Christian group who had humanitarian sympathy for the poor and the oppressed. They were liberal Christians, critical of the conventional churches, and most of them were associated with the Unitarian Association. They were convinced that pacifism, parliamentary procedure, and the organization of labor were the strategic areas for effecting social change. Each participated in social reform as an individual Christian. They lacked any solid sense of unity as a part of the Christian church and any understanding of the church's institutional function in this area. With a liberal understanding of their Christian faith, they clarified little of what is the distinctively Christian way of participating in social movements. Furthermore, their idealism made it impossible for them to be truly relevant to the complex reality of the social situation in which one has both to compromise and to be involved in evil. As government suppression became severe, many of the prominent leaders among the Christian socialists moved to the radical left wing group. On the other hand, some withdrew from the socialist movement and retired from public life. Of the original group of Christian socialists, very few remained in the movement as Christians.

CHRISTIAN INFLUENCE IN THE FRIENDLY SOCIETY

After the Anarchists' Trial of 1911, the government's suppression of the socialist movement increased in vigor, and a general fear of socialism spread widely throughout the country. The socialists tried to continue the movement, but they were unable to widen their influence.

This situation was altered rapidly by World War I, which effected a tremendous change in the structure of Japanese economic life. It quickened the process of industrialization generally and in particular caused the rapid development of heavy industry.

In the Taisho period (1912-25), the revival of the labor movement was led by Bunji Suzuki and others with the establishment of the Friendly Society, which was guided by Clay McCauley of the Unitarian Association. Among the fifteen original members, those from the Unitarian Church assumed the leading positions with Suzuki as president, Isoo Abe as advisor, and Professors Ryo Mikami and Sakusaburo Uchigasaki as committee members. The name Friendly Society was taken over from the Friendly Society of England. Suzuki explained the reason for this: "We shall learn from the lesson of the Friendly Society of England, which aimed at mutual aid, fellowship, and recreation among laborers, and gradually proceeded in the direction of the organization of labor unions, in spite of the pressure of existing laws which limited freedom to organize them."[4]

This then was no radical organization. It took a moderating position and aimed first of all at mutual aid and fellowship among laborers. It sought to bring self-awareness to workers and to reach agreement with managers through reasonable persuasion rather than radical action.

This idea of mutual assistance and co-operation that Suzuki emphasized was based upon his belief in Christian humanism. However, the slow process of co-operation was criticized by some of the members who had been stimulated by the success of the Russian Revolution of 1917.

KAGAWA AND HIS CONTRIBUTION

This was the background against which Toyohiko Kagawa began his lifework by seeking to reform slum conditions in the Shinkawa District of Kobe, and by participating actively in

43

the labor movement in the early part of this century. He occupies in many ways a unique position in the history of social movements in Japan, not only for the broadness of his secular activities, ranging from slum reform and the promotion of agricultural and labor union movements to the co-operative movement, but also for his constant struggles as a Christian leader to rouse the less socially aware among the institutional churches of Japan.

Kagawa is primarily an evangelist who seeks to proclaim plainly, by personal example, the central teaching of Christianity, that God is love. Moreover, he is a man of action. Ideals are not enough; they must be translated into action. Religion is not doctrine but a way of life. Kagawa believes that as Christ offered his life for the sins of others in order to bring the kingdom of God to earth, so it is imperative that Christians sacrifice themselves to eliminate the misery and agony of others. In this sense the advocacy of the Christian message is an economic movement. In turn, an economic movement conducted under this consciousness of the cross is a religious movement. Kagawa cannot accept a dualism separating religion and economics and individual and social morality. Although economics is concerned with material arrangements, its ultimate end is the fulfillment of life.

Although Kagawa is critical of the tendency of the institutional churches to isolate themselves and remain indifferent toward the actual problems of society, he has remained within the church as a minister of a local church and as an evangelist traveling throughout the country.

Kagawa is well known for his work in the slums. As a man who had experienced sorrow from early childhood, he had an irrepressible sympathy for sufferers. After he became a Christian and while severely ill at theological seminary, he became convinced that God had entrusted to him the task of living out the spirit of Christ by working among the poor, spending his life in the slums. In 1909 Kagawa moved into two tiny rooms in the Shinkawa area of Kobe, some of the worst slums in all Japan. There, identifying himself with those in misery and wretchedness, he worked hard to spread the gospel among the people. Early in his work he saw the need for the establishment of a Christian social settlement in the slums. It was not long before the growing group of Christian converts in Shinkawa, with the help of other Christians, were carrying on a wide range of activities, placing evangelism at the center. The program included church services, Sunday school, street preaching, education through an evening school and a sewing school, personal counseling, vocational guidance for the jobless, management of a home for the homeless, a cheap luncheon hall, and a dispensary. Although Kagawa extended his own activities to include the labor unions and the co-operative movement, he and his family remained in Shinkawa, carrying on their work of bringing Christian love to the people of the slums. Later the family moved to Tokyo for relief work. Following the great earthquake of 1923, Kagawa set up a social settlement in the crowded Honjo slum section of Tokyo. After that, through his influence, many other settlements were also started.

The experience of living and working in the slums gave Kagawa firsthand knowledge of the Japanese people and their problems in these blighted areas. While continuing his work in the slums, he came to recognize the limitations of philanthropic projects, which tend to disregard the causes of social disease. He became convinced that without a change in the economic system it was completely hopeless to combat the slum, and he found in labor unions a positive force he believed capable of helping people out of the mire of poverty.

Kagawa participated in the Friendly Society which was developing under the leadership of Bunji Suzuki. In 1919, along with Suzuki and Kozo Kume, Kagawa organized the

Labor Federation of the Friendly Society in the Kwansei area, which includes the cities of Kyoto, Osaka, and Kobe. Kagawa was elected chairman of the board of directors. For Kagawa the function of the labor union is not to win the class struggle nor to obtain job security in the national labor market, but to gain society's protection and respect for the laborer as a human being. He protested against evil factory practices, such as the unhealthy condition surrounding women workers in cotton mills and the high injury rate among laborers. He constantly fought for the revision of the article in the Peace Preservation Law that restricted the formation of labor unions. Through courageous efforts at mediation in various labor-management disputes, Kagawa's leadership became widely recognized. He was invited to give lectures at union meetings, and he became president of two unions in Osaka.

Kagawa also helped organize the All Japan Peasant Union, which sought to aid the farmers to realize the significance of rural life and the necessity of unity to liberate themselves from the bondage of the traditional agricultural society. Within one year this first farmers' union in Japan counted three hundred branches throughout the country and included more than ten thousand members.

In the constant struggle between the right and left wing tendencies within the labor movement, Kagawa consistently sided with the former, standing for parliamentary methods of securing social change rather than direct revolutionary action. He admitted the use of the strike, sabotage, and the boycott, however, on the ground that these are sacrificial acts of labor.

Kagawa took the education of labor seriously and helped in the establishment of labor schools and peasant gospel schools. In his work in the labor movement, his emphasis has been on the enlightenment and education of labor. Although he maintained relations with the Socialist Party both before and after World War II, he has steadfastly refused to become a politician or to become too deeply involved in the sphere of politics. Rather he has assumed a special role as a moral and educational leader in the labor movement.

In spite of the sufferings and difficulties he has encountered through his participation in social movements, Kagawa has constantly looked forward to the future with courage and hope. He presents a picture of the co-operative state as the ideal toward which we should strive. For him the co-operative movement is a means of modifying the vices of capitalism without resorting to revolution. Thus at the same time that he was organizing labor unions, Kagawa was making unbending efforts to develop the co-operative movement.

The comprehensive range of Kagawa's activities is astonishing. The question of depth both with regard to Kagawan theory and Kagawan practice in actual projects may be raised. His discussion often tends to become shallow or sometimes naïve. He has initiated so many projects that he cannot supervise closely the administration of them all. Yet these factors do not detract from his greatness as a sower of the seed of sacrificial love and a pioneer in social movements within the Protestant churches. With his genius, religious insight, and dynamic energy, he still plays a unique role as a courageous leader of Protestantism in Japan.

THE SOCIAL CHRISTIANITY MOVEMENT

From about 1930 to 1940 a group known as Social Christianity was expressing its conviction that the Christian faith was centrally relevant to the social issues of the day. It was most active in the Student Christian Movement and among a group of ministers in the Kwansei area. The movement reflected the social uncertainty and economic depression of the period and was carried forward mainly by students and intellectual leaders.

In spite of varied backgrounds, these leaders shared many

elements in common and looked forward in the same direction. They stood for a dynamic concept of God as the source of creative power and love. The kingdom of God taught by Jesus became the central concern of their theology. The kingdom of God was closely identified with the community of love, which they believed was coming on earth. They did not negate the expectation of a future world; they put the emphasis on the present world in which Christians are called to establish the kingdom of God. In theory, the movement was based on a high estimation of human ability, an optimistic concept of man's sin, and a rather ambiguous idea of the ideal society. In practice, little was developed in the way of a concrete program of social reform.

THE APPROACH OF INSTITUTIONAL CHURCHES

During the critical period after World War I, the churches could by no means remain isolated from the social issues of the day. Among the Protestant churches, the Congregational Churches, which historically have placed more emphasis on the Christian expression of social concern, established a Department of Social Welfare in 1919. Its purpose was to investigate social problems and social work and to conduct an appropriate social program. Although this was the first department among the institutional churches to consider social problems as a special task, the actual activities were greatly limited either by lack of financial support or of participation on the part of local churches. There was no full-time nor part-time secretary to organize the program of the department. According to the annual report, the major project of the year was the support of seven Christian social work centers by raising funds and sending personnel to encourage the work. Being affected by the economic and political crisis of the decade between 1920 and 1930, the other denominations also created departments within their institutional structure, yet the actual programs of these departments were limited merely to the education of the church members. There was little action concerned with the causes of social evils.

One of the significant stands taken by the organized churches during this decade was the Social Creed, which was adopted at the Sixth Assembly of the National Christian Council in November, 1928. It declared:

"Setting up as our ideal a Christian social order in which God is reverenced as Father and humanity interrelated as brothers, we purpose to realize the love, justice, and fraternal oneness manifested by Christ.

"We regret all social reconstruction based on class struggle and revolutionary methods. We are likewise opposed to reactionary oppression. Moreover, taking measures for the extension of Christian education, we pray that many leaders will arise from among us who will pour their lives into the solution of social problems. . . . In conformity with these ideals we advocate the following:

> Equal rights and equal opportunity for all.
> Nondiscriminatory treatment of nationalities and races.
> The sanctity of marriage, equal responsibility of both men and women regarding chastity, and the improvement of home life.
> The betterment of the status of women in the educational, social, political, and industrial worlds.
> Respect for the personality of the child and the prohibition of child labor.
> The enactment of a law making Sunday a public rest day (with the expectation that wages will be paid).
> The abolishment of the system of public prostitution and the complete regulation of all similar trades.
> The promotion of national prohibition.
> The enactment of minimum wage, peasants' welfare, and social insurance laws; and legislation and its implementation, promoting public housing.

49

The encouragement of co-operative associations of producers and consumers.

The establishment of a suitable agency to attain harmonious relations between employees and employers.

The diffusion of a thorough education for working people and the enactment of a reasonable working day.

The enactment of a higher progressive tax rate for income and inheritances.

The limitation of armaments, strengthening of the International Court of Justice, and the realization of a workers' world."[5]

In order to clarify the meaning of the Social Creed, an all-day conference on social problems was held in Tokyo with Kirby Page and Sherwood Eddy as speakers. Between 1928 and 1933, the Kingdom of God Movement under the leadership of Toyohiko Kagawa worked toward the realization of this Social Creed through an evangelistic and educational campaign.

The first Conference on Factory Evangelism in Japan was called in Tokyo on May 10 and 11, 1932, under the joint auspices of the Social Department of the National Christian Council and the Kingdom of God Movement. It was a planning meeting of the Christian factory owners and the church leaders. There were no representatives of Christian laborers in the conference. After expressing his regret over this matter, the general secretary of the National Christian Council said, ". . . but it was inevitable that the number attending be limited in order to avoid unnecessary confusion."[6]

This reflected the feeling of the top leaders of the churches who considered industrial evangelism in terms of a paternalistic approach to labor through Christian managers rather than providing for equal rights for both parties. The institutional church showed almost no concern for organized labor. Thus the emphasis on social concern within the institutional churches had its serious limitations. No real social concern penetrated through to the level of local churches. Rather it was an exchange of opinions among the top leaders. Furthermore, even this exchange lacked both concrete discussion concerning the theological basis of social concern and critical study of the political and economic factors affecting the social issues.

After the Manchurian dispute, even these limited activities carried on by the departments of churches began to fade away. This was a result of the dominating trend toward ultranationalism on the one hand and, on the other hand, the influence of "crisis theology," which was given a very particular interpretation by the theological leaders in the churches.

Within the Protestant churches in the decade of the 1930's, there was a shift of thinking from liberal theology to crisis theology. The leaders of the crisis theology severely criticized the easy harmony of Christ and culture and the optimism often expressed by the Social Christianity group. They advocated the strengthening of church life in which the preaching of the Word of God should take the central place. All their energies were preoccupied with the Word of God in the life of the church, and a dualistic conception of the relation of God and the world precluded any real understanding of the Word of God in the midst of the world.

One of the most crucial points to note in the development of Christian social action in Japan is that the more the level of theological thinking advanced the less social vitality tended to be expressed. As we have seen in the previous chapters, in the early period of the Protestant movement, theological thinking was largely undeveloped in the churches; yet, in terms of actual witness and dynamic action in society, the churches made a remarkable contribution in the midst of a situation of rapid social change. As the churches developed institutional patterns, they tended to adapt themselves to the social environment with an affirmative attitude rather than raising a prophetic witness and criticism against the causes of social evils in the nation.

The crisis theology, instead of providing as it might have done a firm basis for such a prophetic protest, was interpreted in such a way as to deflect the institutional churches even further from such a social witness. Another warning lesson we learn in this regard is exactly the opposite one. It was a tragic matter that Christian leaders in the social reform movements held an optimistic view regarding human progress. They became impatient over the conservative atmosphere of the existing churches and left the churches. Many of them lost the Christian faith that had originally sustained them, and their participation in reform movements lost any distinctively Christian character.

The Postwar Development

One of the new developments in the postwar period is the awareness of the organized churches of past failures, and real efforts have been made to overcome them and to take an active Christian responsibility in society based on genuine theological understanding.

Some of the most urgent tasks of the church in this regard are to clarify the inseparable responsibility of the Christian to serve both God and his neighbor, to formulate courageously the way to render Christian witness in the face of social evils, and to demonstrate Christian concern within the institutional church in such a way as to help the individual Christian to come to his own decision in this area.

The visit of Professor John C. Bennett in 1950 helped the United Church of Christ in Japan to reconsider Christian social responsibility on the basis of the evangelical faith rather than liberal idealism. As a direct result of the national conference with Professor Bennett, the church took a new step in creating the Committee for the Study of Social Problems. Dr. Hidenobu Kuwata, President of Tokyo Union Theological Seminary, who was critical toward the movement of Social Christianity twenty years ago, has now become the chairman of the new committee.

In the postwar period the labor union movement has developed widely and created much discussion. The Committee for the Study of Social Problems issued a statement on the labor movement in Japan from the Christian viewpoint.

First of all, this statement expressed support of the labor union movement. It stated: "The labor union movement, which has been well termed 'the school of democracy,' is of great significance for the democratization of Japan, especially for the democratization of the economic and industrial system and the realization of economic independence. It may fairly be said that the destiny of Japan, now facing a severe crisis, depends upon what happens in the labor movements, which . . . are the central support of the working masses. . . ."

It further stated: "The government instead of hindering and oppressing should encourage the healthy development of the labor union movement as a social force for the establishment of democracy and of economic justice." One of the most important parts in the statement dealt with the radical tendency within the labor unions. In recognizing the fact that the labor union movement in Japan, although suddenly strengthened quantitatively in the postwar period, yet remains very weak in quality, the statement advocated: "The labor movement should be so led that its members will make their place of work, instead of a stage for struggle, a place for co-operation; instead of thinking only of their share in the profits, they will think also of the improvement of their life; instead of thinking only of their advantage as a class, they will think also of the reconstruction of the Fatherland. They must be taught to take seriously their duty together with their rights, their responsibility together with freedom."

The statement concluded with the following words about

the task of the Christian churches: "It is hoped that the Christian church through evangelism, education, and study can render great service [to the development of the labor movement] based upon the Christian spirit instead of class struggle as the church helps to enhance the dignity of the individual and to advance a spirit of toleration and co-operation and an appreciation of social justice and social service."

Since the establishment of the Research Institute on the Mission of the Church within the United Church of Christ in Japan in October, 1955, the Committee for the Study of Social Problems has been functioning as the fourth division of the institute, which takes the relations of church and society as its theme of study.

Another new attempt within the organized churches to relate themselves to an industrial society is the development of occupational evangelism. The United Church of Christ in Japan created a new Committee on Occupational Evangelism in 1950 in order to bridge the gap existing between the church and working class people. Each district has been operating Labor Gospel Schools, and some of these are long-term, higher labor schools that have been attended by hundreds of workers for more than three months in succession. In 1954 the committee invited Henry Jones, a Presbyterian U.S.A. missionary, as a fraternal worker on occupational evangelism. As a resource person in a pioneering field working through the regular program of the churches, he has been making a positive contribution to the development of a Christian witness in an industrial society. This suggests one of the new working patterns for use of missionaries. Christians of other countries with specialized knowledge and rich experience can work with Christians in Japan to help stimulate the churches to an awareness of the challenge of an industrial society, giving direction to the churches and providing some of the means to meet the challenge effectively.

A new attempt has been made in two of the leading theological seminaries, Doshisha Theological School and Kwansei Gakuin Theological School, in the training of future leaders for industrial evangelism. A Seminarian-in-Industry project in the Kwansei area has been started with the help of laymen and ministers who organized the Association to Support Industrial Evangelism (ASIE). As part of this project, one student was assigned to work among seamen in Kobe, another to work in a labor center, another to work among small factories in Kyoto, and another to work with the National Railway Workers' Evangelical Fellowship. In the fall of 1956, Mr. Ochi, of Doshisha, started a new type of work. It is an educational project to train leaders in industrial evangelism to reach workers through music. The whole program has a long-range prospect. It has a uniqueness as an interseminary project that has been undertaken by professors and students together at Doshisha and Kwansei Gakuin.

Another welcome sign in the training of future leaders is the Students-in-Industry project begun under the sponsorship of the National Christian Council of Japan in the summers of 1950 and 1951. It was reopened in the summer of 1956 in Osaka with "Increase of Productivity Movement and Christian Responsibility" as its theme. The students engaged in physical labor and had seminars three nights a week for four weeks. Through this project, Christian young people were brought into an acute awareness of the life situation of the worker and of the immense gap between his world and that of most church members. Many of the students came from rather well-to-do families, and they learned for the first time the ordinary aspects of factory work. One of the surprising things for them was the low wage paid their fellow workers. Simply because they were students, the members of the project received a higher wage than workers doing the same job. The fact that the average wage for the students was three hundred yen per day, or about ten cents an hour, suggests the problem of the low wage system in Japan. Through the project, the students learned the importance of Christian support for legislation to guarantee a fair minimum wage and to protect the rights of laborers.

It is to be hoped that the corporate effort of the churches as a whole will sustain and strengthen activities of the churches such as the organization of study and research as developed in the Research Institute on the Mission of the Church, the provision of opportunities for leadership training as practiced in Seminarian-in-Industry projects and Students-in-Industry projects, and the development of the pioneering ventures in industrial society as tried out in various parts of the country.

The problems arising out of an industrial society are so complex and involve so wide a range of issues that the challenge to the Christian church cannot be met except by the corporate action of all churches. Such action will require the bringing together of personnel, congregations, and physical resources in order to make a common witness in the midst of the urgent needs of society. The call to corporate action by the churches comes not only out of the necessity of the immediate situation. It is also God's purpose for his church "that all may be one." God calls his church to unity in order that it may witness in these times, and he speaks to us both through the Biblical message and the historical situation.

CHAPTER FOUR:

The Church Confronts Nationalism

In an earlier chapter we observed that Christianity came to Japan at the beginning of the modernization of the country and that those who became Christian shared the hope of serving their country with this new religion. An ethical emphasis was strongly evident among them along with patriotic devotion. It was difficult for these early Christians to separate the love of God and love of country. In the early years of the Meiji era, there arose a new sense of belonging to "a nation" and "a people" beyond the divisions of feudal states or the distinctions of feudal classes such as warrior, farmer, craftsman, and merchant. Thus a kind of nationalism arose out of a spontaneous awareness in the minds of the common people that was quite different from the absolute nationalism predominant in later years of the Meiji era, which was inculcated from above with the authority of the state.

In the early period of the Meiji Restoration, there was an intimate connection between the civil liberty movement and Christianity. Many Christians took an active part in the movement. They worked for the development of a democratic and independent nation. Internally they stood for the establishment of a parliamentary system through elections, and externally they strove against domination by foreign powers, evident in the extraterritorial rights and the practice of unbalanced tariffs. The efforts that they made were the efforts to attain freedom; internally they were advocating the freedom of the individual in the political sphere and externally the freedom of their nation in relation to other nations in the world.

They were awakened middle-class liberals who advocated the independence of the nation in order to provide rights for citizens. We may call this democratic nationalism. The nationalism in the later period of the Meiji era, as we shall see, had a different characteristic. It was concerned with the expansion of the rights of the state at the expense of the rights of citizens. We shall call this state nationalism or absolute nationalism.

The spirit of the democratic nationalism was expressed in Hiromichi Kozaki's early work, *A New Theory of Politics and Religion,* published in 1886. Analyzing the contemporary Japanese social situation, Kozaki made a severe criticism of the feudalistic structure of society, which was built upon Confucian teaching. He explained Confucianism as a kind of social law or a practical religion that aims at the peaceful maintenance of order. He pointed out the working method of Confucianism in the following way:

"It has a simple method of achieving its end; it establishes the distinction between the lower and the upper, the noble and the common, those who govern and those who are governed. It helps to establish a kind of society in which those who are in the upper, noble, and governing position have the right to direct the policy, to teach, to establish institutions, and to govern, while those who are in the lower, common, and subordinate positions have the duty to obey the policy, to accept the teaching, and to support the institution. . . . Everyone of the five cardinal virtues of Confucian ethics (except one which defines the relation of friend) concerns the vertical distinction, the distinction between the emperor and the subject, between father and son, between man and wife, and between the old and the young."[1]

Kozaki criticized the feudalistic structure of the Japanese social system, based on Confucian teaching that helped to establish the pyramidal form of society and an authoritarian spirit. He pointed out that the system supported the establishment of absolute monarchy in the state, paternalistic domination of the father in the family, and the authoritarian control of those who govern over those who are governed. He advocated freedom and equality for the individual, explaining that all are sinners before God and, at the same time, all are equally the object of redeeming love. In short, Kozaki made a brave criticism of the hierarchical social system with the absolute power of the Emperor or *Tenno* at the top and feudalistic Japanese morality and clarified the Christian basis for democracy.

This was a revolutionary position in view of the climate of opinion of the early Meiji era. At that time Christianity encountered bitter opposition and persecution because it expressed a courageous criticism of the oppressive and traditional way of life and pointed to a new way. In this sense the Japanese Christian community understood what Christ meant when he said, "I have not come to bring peace but a sword." Christianity was a revolutionary religion!

CHRISTIANS AND THE DEVELOPMENT OF
ABSOLUTE NATIONALISM

As the new government gained centralized control and developed its policy, oppressive tendencies toward the civil liberty movement increased. The government had harrassed the leaders of the civil liberty movement when they came to Tokyo to make three petitions: one for treaty revision, one for reduction of land taxes, and the third for freedom of speech and assembly. Finally the government passed the Peace Preservation Law in December, 1887. In Article IV the civil liberty movement leaders were condemned as persons who stirred up public discord and planned civil war.

59

The government restricted the popular movement for freedom, while from above it appeared to give freedom. This was symbolized by the Constitution of 1889, which was acclaimed as a gift to the people from the Emperor. However, the adoption of a constitution was due partly to the government's policy of Westernization. It provided a constitutional and legal system comparable to those of Occidental countries, and the government hoped that its adoption would favorably impress the Western powers with whom Japan was negotiating to revise the old inequitable treaties. The constitution took the Western form of a constitutional monarchy, yet in its heart it declared, "The Emperor is sacred and inviolable," and at its roots the hierachical structure was presupposed. A benevolent emperor was the head, and the subjects were required to give him obedience and loyalty.

For Christians, who had been regarded as a sort of ruined people, it was of great concern to know the attitude of the constitution toward religion. It stated: "Japanese subjects shall, within limits not prejudicial to peace and order and not antagonistic to their duties as subjects, enjoy freedom of religious belief." Although this was a religious freedom that was conditioned and limited by national duties as subjects of the state, the declaration gave great assurance and joy to those Christians who had been persecuted and had fought for the maintenance of religious liberty.

Few of them were aware of the dangers hidden in the external Western dress of the constitution. It was ironical that when the nation was celebrating the constitution on February 11, 1889, Viscount Mori Arinori, the Minister of Education, was assassinated by a conservative nationalist because he was regarded as a Christian and an advocate of Westernization. Although he was not actually a Christian, he was a progressive leader. The event well exemplifies the evil of the absolute nationalistic tendency, which can be distinguished from the democratic nationalism of the earlier period.

It was against this background that on October 30, 1890, the Emperor issued the Imperial Rescript on Education, which set forth the basic ethical principles for his subjects who were to accept it as "the teaching requested by our Imperial Ancestors to be observed alike by their descendants and subjects, infallible for all ages and true in all places."[2]

In the Rescript, Shinto ideology was combined with ethical Confucianism and expressed in a framework of Western morality. Morality was founded on loyalty to the Emperor and filial piety. The feudalistic hierarchical structure was to be maintained in a centralized modern state, headed by the Emperor as absolute authority of the nation.

Moreover, it is important to understand the authority of the Rescript as well as the content. Copies of it were sent to the schools, students were urged to memorize it, and on certain national holidays the teachers and pupils gathered together in the auditorium to listen to its reading. A missionary described all this in the following words: "It is taken in the most reverential way from the box in which it is kept, slowly unrolled, and read to the members of the school, who stand with bowed heads as they listen to the august words of their Emperor. The slightest lack of decorum is looked upon as almost treasonable."[3] The Rescript was regarded as something holy and authoritative because it came from the Emperor. In this period, the Emperor had moved gradually from absolute ruler to divine authority, a sort of living god-man.

Kanzo Uchimura had to resign from the First High School in Tokyo because he was accused by the nationalists of having shown disrespect to the Rescript. The incident was exaggerated by the press, and Christian churches were attacked by nationalistic educational leaders. Furthermore, a similar tendency was encouraged regarding the attitude toward the picture of the Emperor. On national holidays the pupils of schools bowed reverently before the picture of the Emperor.

Thus the government not only built the political structure of modern Japan with the support of the financial oligarchy and the aristocrats, but it also constructed a spiritual basis that would integrate all aspects of national life with a semi-religious devotion. In the early days of the Meiji era, Christians were persecuted as antisocial since they opposed the feudalistic teaching of the old society. Now, with the emergence of the Tenno system, Christians were accused of being antinational since they claimed in the Christian God an authority superior to the Emperor.

Christian churches faced difficulties during this period. Despite the increase in the number of new missionaries from 434 in 1888 to 646 in 1894, the numbers of new Christians declined from 7,387 to 2,854. The mission schools, which were rapidly established during the period of Westernization, suffered a great deal in this period of growing nationalism.

As to why the churches did not make progress, in spite of the fact that religious freedom was granted in the constitution, several reasons may be pointed out. The first is the reactionary and nationalistic tendency of this period described above. The second is that within the churches there were reactions to the superficial period of Westernization. With the tide of the period, churches that had expanded beyond their capacity now found their work hard to maintain. In some cases there were unreliable and unstable characteristics in the revival movement so that the programs of the churches tended to be carried on temporarily and on a short-term basis rather than with a long-term perspective. The third element was that there was an uncertainty within the churches as to their theological basis after the introduction of the so-called "new" liberal theology that came from Germany and the United States.

In 1885 the Allgemeine Evangelisch-Protestantische Missions Verein came to Japan. This new missionary venture arose originally as a criticism of a narrow, dogmatic Christianity and demanded a broadened basis to unite the various theological parties and stressed a Christianity in which faith and science were reconciled.

From America the Unitarian Association started its mission in 1888, and Universalists also sent missionaries to Japan in 1890. In 1891 Kanamori published a small book entitled *The Present and the Future of Christianity in Japan,* in which he accepted the liberal criticism of the Bible and criticized orthodox Protestantism. The journal, *Rikugo Zasshi,* published by the Y.M.C.A., became an instrument of liberal theological opinion at this time. In the wake of this theological storm, some of the prominent ministers like Yokoi and Kanamori left church activity and entered business and political fields. Many of the less educated members of the church who were not acquainted with the theological issues were stunned by the defection of their pastors. Their action seemed to be an admission that what they had taught was wrong.

Responding to the tide of nationalism in society, there arose efforts to correlate the Christian faith with the nationalistic spirit of the time, and the new liberal theology lent itself to such efforts. In 1890 Tokio Yokoi discussed "The Future of Christianity in Japan" in the following way:

"The Christianity which was practiced in our country was the Christianity of the West. The theology of our churches and our Christian living have been following the examples of Western countries. We have very few who can be called Japanese Christians. From now on there is an opportunity to develop genuine Christianity in the Japanese spirit. Western Christianity has developed with the aid of Greek literature and Roman law. Christianity which is going to rise in the East has to be built on the basis of Buddhistic or Confucianistic culture, combining and developing the goodness and beauty which exist among them."

In the midst of the general criticism of Christian churches,

63

which were regarded as a sort of foreign colony by the nationalists and reactionaries of the time, the liberals made an effort to defend themselves and tried to show that devotion to the nation was as great within the churches as outside the churches. Yokoi concluded with these words: "In view of the present situation, Christianity will not secure the Christianization of our country unless it takes off the dress which came from abroad and becomes a part of our national life."[4]

The effort to express Christianity within the framework of the genuine national uniqueness should not be condemned. It is rather an encouraging tendency and should be welcomed. But the vital question confronting us here is how and in what form this effort should take place. And furthermore, what is the ultimate intention in such an attempt? It was rather unfortunate that the effort to develop an indigenous Japanese expression of Christianity was made within a narrow national perspective rather than with the recognition of diversity in form and practice in the one world-wide fellowship of the Christian community.

As the nationalistic spirit was intensified, Kanamori emphasized Japanese Christianity and expressed a critical view of foreign missionaries; Ebina tried to correlate Christianity with Shinto morality; Yokoi made an effort to harmonize Confucianism and Christianity; and Iichiro Tokutomi, who was formerly considered an advocate of democracy, came to favor omnipotent imperialism. Even Kozaki, who formerly expressed critical opinions of the Tenno system, made the following remark: "There is a valid tendency which was evident in this reactionary period, namely the effort to integrate the spirit of the nation. We agree with the tendency and should make all our efforts aim for the development of it. Now our country is facing the time for building a new nation."[5]

An important factor in fanning the flames of absolute nationalism, not only in the Meiji period but even to the present

64

day, has been the unequal trade agreements and tariff practices which Japan has been forced to accept. Discriminatory tariff practices by other nations not only hit at the pocketbooks of the nation but also at its pride. Such tariff practices struck at a vulnerable spot for a nation troubled by overpopulation combined with insufficient farm lands and natural resources. In many cases the unequal tariffs were imposed ostensibly because of the low level of wages paid to Japanese workers, which meant goods produced in Japan could undersell those of other countries. However, such wages were the result of a comparatively low standard of living, which could be raised only through the sale overseas of manufactured articles for which the bulk of the raw materials was secured abroad. When free access to raw materials and markets was denied, the only alternatives before Japan were to depress wages further or by military conquest to gain control of the sources of raw materials and markets.

This fact has strengthened the hands of the absolute nationalists in carrying out successive campaigns for domination of areas of the Asian mainland. In more recent years the problem of tariffs has become more crucial, for it is now estimated that not more than 80 per cent of the food necessary for Japan can be produced domestically. It is necessary for Japan to trade or receive foreign aid to make possible purchases of food from abroad if her ninety million people are to be fed. Christian ethics would seem to match with Japanese desire for access to markets that would enable the country to supply the needs of her people.

The tendency toward absolute nationalism was accelerated when the nationalistic spirit of the country was whipped up by the Sino-Japanese War (1894-95) and the Russo-Japanese War (1904-05). In both cases the Christians had an opportunity to prove their loyalty to the nation and disprove the charge of being nonnationalistic that had been raised against them. During the war periods, Christians united to

65

form a special association which engaged in various tasks such as serving in hospitals and army camps, sending booklets to soldiers, and giving moral support to the war. Christian soldiers, who formerly were discriminated against by the military authorities, were now given an opportunity to serve the nation in this way, too. With few exceptions, Christians participated uncritically in the wars. The basis for their participation was largely the concept of a just war.

During the war against Russia, Christians were suspected by the public of being un-co-operative since Russia was professedly a Christian nation. Kozaki, as the representative of the Christian churches, made an address at the General Meeting of Adherents of All Religions on the purpose of the war, in which he said:

"This war is neither between races nor religions. It may indeed be considered a war between the civilization of the sixteenth century and that of the twentieth century, for Russia represents the civilization of the sixteenth as our country represents that of the twentieth century. . . .

"In rendering service to our country, the adherents of all religions should be closely united and should become, as it were, one huge cannon ball to protect the country."[6]

With their nationalistic background, the Christians could not remain detached while the nation faced a crisis. They were not critical of the over-all absolutist policies of the Meiji government, but they uncritically rejoiced over the religious freedom provided by the constitution, although it was conditional. They expressed their support of the war and, in turn, received the approval of the government.

CHRISTIANITY AND PACIFISM

Although in the institutional churches there was little evidence of an antiwar position, there were, of course, exceptions. For example, Kinosuke Shiraishi of Kakegawa, in discussing the war in *Gokyo,* a Methodist journal, said:

"Do not say that war is a means to bring permanent peace. The end cannot justify the means. A man who steals in order to give cannot escape from the punishment of law. War is evil. Therefore, God never uses war as a means to manifest his great will, namely the salvation of the world. . . . The special tasks of Christianity are to proclaim the brotherhood of man, to modify hatred of the enemy, to reduce the evils of war by appealing to humanity. In contrast, the leaders of the churches are praising the war by compromising with the secular trends and are increasing more and more the crisis of the day."[7]

Another remarkable Christian pacifist during the Russo-Japanese War was Kanzo Uchimura. Although he had supported the Sino-Japanese War on the grounds of the just-war theory, at the time of the Russo-Japanese War he took a pacifist position and said: "I am not only opposed to the outbreak of the war against Russia but also against any kind of war. War is to kill. And killing is a great sin. Neither the individual nor the state is able to profit out of such sinful acts."[8]

He based his conviction upon Biblical teachings that denounced resistance, such as, "Do not resist one who is evil," and "Blessed are the meek, for they shall inherit the earth." On certain occasions he criticized war from a practical point of view, though with high idealism. In most cases he advocated pacifism from his conviction based on a literal interpretation of the commandments of nonresistance in the New Testament rather than on a realistic examination as to the cause and result of a specific war.

After his resignation from *Yorozu,* the largest newspaper in Japan, Uchimura took up the teaching of the Bible as his life calling. He continued the publication of *Seisho no Kenkyu* (Study of the Bible) until his death in 1930. All social problems according to Uchimura were reduced to religious problems, and the Bible provided the source for the solution of

67

these. In regard to social issues, he took the Bible seriously on two grounds. The first was the conviction that, since social reform depends on the changes of the individual's soul, the Bible is the essential source for the regeneration of society through the individual. The second was that the moral teachings of the Bible, particularly the commandments of Jesus, were to be taken directly for application to social problems.

Just as he took his own work as a calling, so Uchimura encouraged his disciples to take seriously their secular work as a vocation by emphasizing the priesthood of all believers and opposing the traditional ecclesiastical order. In the "Non-Church" associations for Bible study and Christian fellowship that Uchimura founded, there were no clergy nor formal organization.

It should be made clear that Uchimura, in spite of his pacifist stand, was essentially and constantly a patriot. He expressed strongly his criticism of foreign missionaries and encouraged Japanese Christians to maintain independence both spiritually and financially. As he accepted the gospel in samurai soil, Uchimura and his disciples were interested in making Christianity a Japanese religion rather than an imported foreign religion.

Although Uchimura touched on several of the social issues of the day, like the Ashio Mine dispute, socialism, and Japanese-American problems in 1924, the problem he was constantly concerned with was the issue of war. It is not an exaggeration to say that he made the issue of war and peace a single issue strategy. He was little concerned with a rational examination of war and its cause and effect; he started with the conviction that war is evil and advocated absolute pacifism. In his later period, the emphasis shifted to the second coming of Christ, claiming he alone is able to bring eternal peace. Here again, for Uchimura, the teaching of the Bible to each individual became the important method while waiting for Christ's coming.

There were other examples of Christian pacifism represented in men like Gien Kashiwagi, who held that pacifism is the vocation of religious leaders, and Kiyoshi Yabe, pastor of Zeze Church, who was put into prison because he was a conscientious objector at the time of the Russo-Japanese War. The constant effort made by the Society of Friends in promoting peace through the Japan Peace Society, which they established in 1890, should also be noted.

THE ATTITUDE OF THE ORGANIZED CHURCH

Corresponding to the nationalistic trend of the time, the independence movement rapidly made progress among Japanese churches. By the independence movement is meant the drive to be self-governing and self-supporting. The decision to be independent of the missions was arrived at by the Congregational Churches in the General Council of 1894, and the actual plan was enacted by 1905. According to their plan, the Congregational American Board of Commissioners for Foreign Missions would provide a sum of 8,700 yen within three years in order to help forty-seven churches and sixteen preaching centers to become independent without further claim upon the mission. The Japanese Home Mission Society raised 9,600 yen to assist nonselfsupporting churches.

The independence of the Presbyterian Church in Japan, of the Japan Methodist Church, and of the Anglican Church in Japan also took place at about the same time. Although the desire to be independent and self-supporting probably existed from the beginning, the Russo-Japanese War and the nationalistic spirit it engendered gave it further impetus.

After the Russo-Japanese War, nationalistic tendencies in Japan continued to be strong, but general social unrest increased. In the cabinet, Takejiro Tokonami became the Vice-Minister of the Home Ministry. He had previously made a trip to the West and was impressed with the wide influence of Christianity. On his return he proposed a conference of three religions, Shintoism, Buddhism, and Christianity, in order to gain the co-operation and support of all three in effectively fostering national spirit. On February 25 and 26, 1912, representatives from all three religions met in Tokyo and at the end of two days passed the following resolutions:

"I. We will severally exert ourselves in the propagation of our own doctrine for the enhancement of the prestige of the Imperial House and the gradual increase of the morality of the nation.

"2. We hope that the Home Department officials will respect religion so that harmony between the government, religion, and education may be attained in a manner to aid the national destiny."[9]

The majority of the leaders of the churches welcomed this development and expressed their willingness to support the resolutions made at the meetings. Thus the Christian leaders responded favorably rather than being critical of the strong underlying nationalistic development. They were pleased by the government's recognition of the Christian churches as equal to the two other religions, and, in turn, they pledged themselves to co-operate with national policies through spiritual and moral support. Within the Protestant churches, few spoke against the trend. The prophetic and critical spirit of the Christian leaders of the early Meiji era was gradually dimming.

Masahisa Uemura, one of the most influential leaders of the Presbyterian stream, was not satisfied with the developments of the meeting. He insisted upon the separation of church and state. Moreover, he began to withdraw from participation in the affairs of the public world and concentrated on the training of members of the church. He was not an isolationist nor an individualist, but he concentrated on building a strong church through which he intended to train members to serve society.

Unlike Uchimura, who criticized the institutional church,

Uemura exalted the worth of the existing church. Throughout his life he constantly endeavored to make the preaching of the gospel the central task of the church. He accepted the Pauline emphasis of *kerygma* rather than the ethical teachings of Tolstoy.

It is interesting to note Uemura's attitude toward the three trends among the Japanese Protestant churches of his time. One trend was a group developing along nationalistic lines, objecting to foreign aid and seeking support from native Japanese sources. Directly opposed were groups completely in favor of co-operation with foreign missions through whose support they intended to expand their power. Finally, there were those who adopted the strategy of concentration on the building of strong churches in order to expand their influence gradually throughout the land.

Although Uemura did not explicitly take sides, one would not be far amiss in regarding him as an advocate of the third position. In recognizing the limitation involved in the third position, he made the following remarks in which he pointed out some dangerous pitfalls confronting this group: "Those who belong to this group have a strong desire to know nothing but Christ and His crucifixion. . . . As one negative consequence, they tend to be blind to the over-all picture and lack a positive program. They are apt to shut themselves up within their churches, becoming defensive at the challenge of society. There is a danger of their becoming fossilized."[10]

The government's policy of fostering co-operation among the different religious groups was actively continued from the turn of the century on. As the nationalistic tendency increased, the government tried to combine and control religious forces and utilize them for promoting its national aims. Furthermore, the government asserted that state Shinto was a national moral practice rather than a religion and that its rituals should be observed throughout the country. One of these, called the National Ceremony, was a brief ceremony of prayer for those who had died in battle and a bow in the direction of the Emperor's palace. This was practiced not only in public schools but also in the churches.

In 1930 the National Christian Council of Japan made statements protesting against the government policy, insisting that if Shinto was not a religion it should do away with its religious practices. However, the government disregarded the protest and increased the further enforcement of Shinto practices at most official meetings.

Governmental pressure further increased after the beginning of war with China in April, 1938. For instance, the military police in Osaka sent questionnaires to the ministers in the city to inquire about their attitude on the relation between the teachings of state Shinto and Christianity. They raised such points as the relation between God and Tenno (the Emperor or Ruler of Heaven), the relation between the Bible and the Imperial Rescript, and the attitude toward the practice of worship at shrines.

The government control of religions came about through the Law for the Control of Religious Organizations that passed the Diet in 1938. It aimed at providing protection and controls for religious organizations and set up much stricter regulations regarding their relation to public peace and welfare. The new law provided three grounds on which the Minister of Education or a local governor could order the suspension or dismissal of a person holding office in any religious organization: ". . . the specific violation of written law and ordinance, conduct that the competent minister of state judges harmful to public welfare, and finally actions that are judged to contravene the regulations of the particular religious body as drawn up by that body and approved by the authority of the government."[11] Thus the government was in a position to require support from the churches in mobilizing the spiritual forces of the nation in a time of crisis.

CHAPTER FIVE:

The Task of the Church
in a Divided World

The Law for the Control of Religious Organizations served as a goad to the movement toward church unity, the origin of which was in the formation of the first church in Japan on a nondenominational basis. More recent expressions of this movement have been the merged church life of what elsewhere would be separate denominations. In October, 1940, thirty-four denominations decided to form the United Church of Christ in Japan, which held its first assembly in June, 1941. At first this union was considered as a semifederated church made of eight "blocks," each composed of former denominations with a similar heritage. After a year, it became an organically merged church as it continues today. It is significant that the United Church of Christ in Japan has grown in its sense of unity and mission, but it should be noted that following the end of World War II, the Anglican, Lutheran, Southern Baptist, Reformed, Church of Christ, the Free Methodists, and certain other evangelical churches withdrew to form separate denominations.

CHRISTIAN CHURCHES DURING WORLD WAR II

As the relation between Japan and the Western countries became critical, government suspicion and oppression were inevitably directed toward the Christian community. The

73

leaders of the Salvation Army were arrested in August, 1940, under the accusation of espionage through their routine reports to their London headquarters. The threat of similar action against the Anglican and Protestant Episcopal leaders accelerated the separation of the churches from their missionary relationships. The churches were directed to reduce the number of their missionary personnel and to cut down financial relations with the Western churches. By the summer of 1941, out of a total that had reached nearly one thousand, scarcely one hundred Protestant foreign missionaries remained in Japan.

At this time, hoping to promote better understanding, the National Christian Council of Japan proposed talks with American Christians. Eight delegates were sent to the United States, and a conference with seventeen American church leaders was held at Riverside, California. Similar meetings were held at Atlantic City, New Jersey, and Chicago, Illinois. Although these encounters could not change the total situation, which was already moving fast in the direction of war, yet they underlined the fact that until the end Christians sought to understand one another. Such efforts to be more effective should be widened and deepened at earlier stages in situations where there is any danger of a developing conflict.

After the outbreak of the war, the churches were assigned tasks related to national spiritual mobilization. They emphasized Japan's high ethical ideals in carrying on the war. Through lectures, the teaching of young people and adults, and conferences, the Christians participated in the war as in some sense a holy war. It was not defensive for the protection of the nation but was regarded positively because they felt Japan had a "manifest destiny" for the liberation of Asia through the war and the establishment of the Greater Asian Circle. Urged by government authorities to co-operate, churches with few exceptions took an active part in the war effort through the Wartime Christian Service Association, sending packages to the troops, giving for the war, promoting national savings, giving direction to wartime living, sponsoring thrift campaigns, undertaking religious propaganda in Asia, and praying for victory.

During the war the Holiness Church and the Seventh Day Adventists suffered at the hands of the government because of their religious convictions. Both groups were extreme literalists in their interpretation of the Bible and preached without compromise the physical second coming of Christ as judge with the end of the present organization of society. This immediately caused conflict with the absolute Tenno idea. All forty-one leaders of the Holiness Church were arrested and put into prison. Suffering from bad conditions, especially lack of sanitation, overcrowding, and bad food, eight of them died either during the prison term or soon after release.

All forty-two ministers and key lay leaders of the Seventh Day Adventists were similarly arrested. Their sentences ranged from acquittal to four-year imprisonment. The last six still serving sentence were released after the end of the war. When they were freed, all but nine of the original forty-two were ill, and four died soon afterward.

There were also individual Christians who stood firmly against the war as conscientious objectors. Although such efforts were limited by the fact that they were individualistic and fragmental, they provided a courageous and conscientious witness in the midst of hysterical support for the war.

As the war became severe and destruction widespread, churches did not escape the devastation striking all around them. The total losses approximated one-fourth of all the church properties in Japan and were distributed throughout the country. But in its effect the loss was even greater since most of the churches destroyed were in the centers of population and influence. Of the 169 Protestant church buildings in Tokyo, only nine were left standing. The case of the moderator of the General Assembly of the United Church is typical of the plight of many of the church leaders as the war neared its close. He was the pastor of a church with about one hundred and fifty families. The same bombings that destroyed the church and parsonage also burned the homes of all but seven of these families. Thus the parish itself was destroyed and the congregation scattered and homeless, many of them having to leave the city. It is estimated that at the close of the war the total Christian community of some 350,000 persons had been reduced by about one half. The Christian movement had sustained a serious setback, but it had kept the faith and had lived through.

POSTWAR RECONSTRUCTION

On August 15, 1945, after the destruction of Hiroshima and Nagasaki, Japan surrendered. The message of the surrender from the Emperor was broadcast throughout the nation. The shadow of dark days had passed, and in the midst of ruin and ashes a new chapter for Japan had begun. One of the remarkable aspects of the reconstruction of Japan was the ingenuity and diligence of the Japanese in struggling with hardship and suffering. It is almost equally true that the rapid recovery that they have achieved would have been impossible without the sympathy and help that the Occupation authority and the people of the United States and Canada provided.

This also applies to the reconstruction of Christian institutions, which has been accomplished through the combined effort of Japanese Christians, working diligently and often sacrificially, and of Christians in other lands, generously giving aid. In the summer of 1947, a deputation visited Japan representing the Foreign Missions Conference of North America, which included the mission boards of most of the denominations. As one result, a goal was adopted for the reconstruction of two hundred church buildings. Four years later, 228 of the destroyed church buildings of the United Church of Christ in Japan had been rebuilt. The Japanese churches raised at least 10 per cent of the cost of reconstructions, often more. Often, moreover, the largest part of the remaining fund came through the Interboard Committee for Christian Work in Japan, composed of the mission boards of the following churches that co-operate as they work with the United Church of Christ in Japan: Congregational Christian, Disciples of Christ, Evangelical and Reformed, Evangelical United Brethren, Methodist, Presbyterian Church U.S.A., Reformed, and United Church of Canada.

All other denominations not within the United Church of Christ in Japan carried on similar programs of reconstruction with assistance from abroad. By now the task of rebuilding the destroyed churches is almost completed, and churches are ready to undertake new projects.

As Professor Arnold Toynbee has pointed out, one of the vital new facts of this century is that men have learned to help one another in time of need. This was certainly true in the case of the reconstruction of ruined Japan. One of the remarkable demonstrations of such help in time of need was the work of LARA (Licensed Agencies for Relief in Asia), which was organized in the spring of 1946. With the co-operation of Occupation officials, LARA was organized as a joint committee composed of representatives of such agencies as: American Friends Service Committee, Brethren Service Committee, Church World Service (representing the co-operative relief effort of many American denominations), Lutheran World Relief, Mennonite Central Committee, Catholic War Relief Services, and the National Catholic Welfare Conference.

Through LARA relief supplies were distributed to persons in carefully selected categories on the basis of need without respect to religious affiliation. Food was still rationed by the government after the war, but the distributed ration allowed less than half of the minimum required daily calories, about 1,400 calories. Many times the rations were not regularly distributed, were delayed for a month, or in the worst cases there simply were no rations at all for several weeks. In this situation among the various special needs, three were decided upon as most urgent: food for war waifs, milk for babies whose mothers could not nurse them, and extra rations for tuberculosis patients of whom there seemed to be an alarming number. With the ardent efforts of the committee, the program grew until it included food for "about 20,000 children in institutions in all prefectures, milk for 10,000 babies each month, extra rations for 60,000 T.B. patients in sanatoria, 60,000 day nursery children, 30,000 university students, and 30,000 sick persons served by health centers."[1]

In 1952, after remarkable service, LARA went out of existence. However, because it was felt strongly by social welfare leaders and social service institutions in Japan that the need was still present for relief supplies sent by Christian people abroad, a continuing committee was formed called CAC, using the first initials of the co-operating agencies: Church World Service, American Friends Service Committee, and Catholic War Relief Services. Also serving on this CAC Committee are Japanese representatives from the National Council of Social Work and the Japanese Ministry of Welfare. CAC has continued to be actively engaged in relief and rehabilitation work and has helped meet the urgent human needs caused by disasters such as floods in the south, unemployment in the mining areas, and famine in Hokkaido.

Another important agency whose work cannot be overlooked is CARE. CARE began the distribution of food packages in July, 1948. Gift food packages were sent to needy individuals not covered by the LARA program. Up to the end of June, 1950, food and other types of relief packages distributed by CARE totaled 72,573. It is impossible to estimate the number of relief packages that have been sent from church groups in America to individuals whose names have been forwarded by Christian workers in Japan, but it was stated by the postal authorites that nearly $2,000,000 worth of relief supplies entered Japan through personal packages delivered during the first two years after mail service opened.[2] All of these relief supplies have been appreciated deeply by Japanese recipients, both for the actual material assistance that they brought and for the spiritual concern that they symbolized. Through this aid an old friendship that had been broken on both sides of the Pacific has been renewed and enriched.

RECONCILIATION THROUGH THE CHRISTIAN MOVEMENTS

After the years of restriction and oppression, there is a feeling of freedom and openness in Japan today. But spiritual reconstruction is far more complex and problematic than is the physical reconstruction of the country. Two catchwords characterize the spiritual condition of postwar Japan—freedom and peace. After the unhappy experience under the harsh restrictions of an ultranationalist government and the traditional oppression of individual personality by a feudalistic society, freedom was the term that caught the imagination of many people. The idea of democracy, with differing connotations, was accepted by many Japanese, and as part of democracy economic freedom (especially for attaining one's economic security) and freedom of expression of political opinion and religious faith were both advocated ardently. The emphasis rested mainly upon freedom from bondage and restriction rather than freedom for participation with commitment.

To fight against existing injustice and oppression is only half of the struggle for freedom. Real freedom is positive. The vital question that confronts those in search of freedom lies in what kind of participation and personal commitment real freedom is to be found. A significant battle for the loyalties of men is being waged around the meaning of freedom in Japan today. The Christian faith has a profound relevance for this search for real freedom. Marxists as well as many others are in the arena. The Christian faith provides us with an understanding of the will of God for justice and community among men. It frees man to enter the struggle against injustice and bondage. The full freedom for participation and commitment comes in the realization of the fact of being accepted by the unwarranted love of God, who is the source of existence as well as the power that overcomes evil and bondage.

It is a widely recognized fact that there are strong tendencies among Japanese young people to claim freedom from existing social bondage and traditional norms and to take only themselves as the positive ground of participation with no ultimate point of reference, no source of judgment and renewal. As a result they find themselves captive to self, in slavery to an egocentric structure. There is an immeasurable need and opportunity to bring the Christian message to those who thus are in urgent search of real freedom.

The second catchword in Japan today is peace. After the repeated and bitter experience of war, there is a wide and genuine desire for peace in postwar Japan. The search for peace is the response to an urgent cry that came from many student-soldiers who lost their lives in battle. The wish for peace is not a sentimental vision but a real prayer that was born in many of those who experienced directly the ruin and tragedy of the war. Christians have a vital role to play in this situation as peacemakers who will create better understanding, break down the dividing wall of hostility, and bring about reconciliation.

Participation in conferences held in the circle of the world Christian community has helped to widen perspective and has provided the opportunity for re-establishing fellowship that had been broken. Although Japan could not send representatives to the World Christian Youth Conference held at Oslo in 1947, fraternal messages were exchanged. Japanese churches, however, were able to send a delegate to the First Assembly of the World Council of Churches held in Amsterdam the following year. As postwar reconstruction developed, it became increasingly possible to take a part in international conferences. The Student Christian Movement sent delegations to the World's Student Christian Federation conferences in Ceylon in 1948, Travancore in South India in 1952, and Tutzing in Germany in 1956. These occasions symbolized the oneness of the world Christian fellowship, widened the scope of mutual understanding, and held out the challenge of reconciliation in a divided world.

Japanese student participants at these world conferences sought to share with fellow Christian students from other lands their concern for the achievement of true peace, freedom, and democracy. They sought out delegates from nations whose policies were felt to hinder the realization of these goals in Japan and the world at large. As students from a nation that had known the terror of thought-control police, they were particularly anxious about threats to academic freedom and asked, "Does not the Christian imperative to know the truth mean that we must strive for freedom of expression for even the Marxist professor?" With extreme poverty as the constant companion of most students and faced with the fact that a substantial number of graduates could not find employment, they raised questions as to the meaning of democracy for the economic welfare of men. Believing that the adequate provision of bread for others is a Christian ethical concern, they asked, "Is not socialism the best solution to the economic problems of Asian have-not nations?" Coming from a nation that is extremely sensitive to racial discrimination, they raised their voices over the economic causes behind various unjust racial practices.

The tragedy that World War II brought to Japan caused

Japanese students to ask, "In seeking peace for the world, as ambassadors of reconciliation is not our role to avoid the commitment of our nation to either side in the cold war and rather make efforts, along with other Asian nations, to reduce international tension by the creation of a third force?" Those who asked questions were also particularly articulate about the outlawing of nuclear weapons, maintenance of the Japanese Peace Constitution, and the withdrawal from Japan of American troops, all of which will be discussed in this chapter.

Various international projects held in Japan have also provided a unique opportunity for fellowship and service. The first international work camps were organized under the sponsorship of the Youth Department of the World Council of Churches in 1949. Every year since then, both international work camps and youth caravans have been organized in various parts of the country. In order to renew the fellowship once broken by the war, the United Church of Christ in the Philippines sent a good-will team of young people to Japan in 1954. They visited the major cities in Japan. The team helped to create a better understanding between Japanese and Filipinos and to promote the spirit of reconciliation in Christ.

In the spring of 1957, four Japanese students were sent to the Philippines, where two participated in the Asian Conference on Christian Journalism held at Manila and two took part in an international work camp that engaged in rural reconstruction work in a Bataan village called Mabatang, which had seen some of the bitterest fighting during the war.

By the invitation of the Christian movement in China, a good-will team of twelve men and three women, representing interdenominational Christian groups, made a visit to Communist China in the spring of 1957 with a sincere spirit of reconciliation and desire for mutual understanding. These and many other such projects of international Christian movements have provided a valuable opportunity for encounter and reconciliation. As Christians we are called upon to love others as Christ loved us. Thus one of the urgent tasks of Christians in this divided world is to act as the bridge of understanding, as Christ reconciled us to God.

THE PROBLEMS AND WAYS OF PEACE

The mere wish for peace is not enough. The demand of the gospel is that Christians act as peacemakers. Just to exchange happy greetings and good words is not difficult; the real task is to face actual problems and, on the basis of better understanding and mutual faith, take positive action. It is true that there is a nationwide desire for peace existing in postwar Japan. A few tend to idealize peace, taking either a sentimental attitude or an absolute position toward peace; others may play the term peace as political strategy. For most Japanese, however, peace is the genuine expression both of the desire of the individual and of what they believe to be the historical mission of their nation after the experince of a bitter and tragic war.

The new constitution, formulated in 1946, crystallized this wide concern for peace. It has been called the Peace Constitution since it renounces war. In the Ninth Article, it renounces both aggressive and strategic war, and it forbids the actual use or threat of military forces as a means of settling international disputes. Consequently the constitution does not allow the possession of land, sea, and air forces nor any kind of war potential; thus it completely abandons the right of belligerency. The constitution was the product of a unique combination of the will of the Japanese to be a peaceful nation and the insistence of the Allied Forces that Japan should not rearm. There are some Japanese who believe that the present constitution is a "given constitution" in the sense that it has been imposed upon the Japanese by the Allied

Forces as victors. Nevertheless, the reluctance to rearm is far too widespread to be either Communist inspired or the result of an Occupation policy. It is a genuine expression of Japanese feeling.

Such an attitude reflects a high moral ideal. It also presents real difficulties for maintaining security without force in the midst of international tension and struggle. Japan entered the United Nations in 1956, and within this framework she may be able to make a significant witness for peace while, at the same time, she is accorded security and understanding as a member nation.

The following statement, signed by seven of the outstanding intellectual leaders of Japan, is representative of opinion generally:

"Japan should appeal to the nations that she wishes to preserve this constitution and ask that they take steps promptly to begin to bring their policies in line with the ideal of attaining peace and security without arms and by renouncing the rights of belligerency. Japan might thus become the outspoken champion of the necessity of world disarmament with the advantage that she is the first country to have a constitutional basis for such a program. As envisaged in the Atlantic Charter, the world must come eventually to the renunciation of the use of force in international relations. Some countries must take the lead in the implementation of this policy. Vigorous moral leadership on the part of Japan in that direction might make a very significant contribution to world peace."

In this connection the problem of military bases should be mentioned. Under the Mutual Security Pact, signed between the United States and Japan, the United States forces occupy military bases throughout the country. This causes many problems. The first of these is the economic problem related to the farmers whose lands were taken for the bases or to fishermen whose supply of fish decreased because of bombing tests.

The second problem comes from lack of understanding Japanese sensitivity. For instance, in the spring of 1955, the United States Army set its artillery practice range on the very slopes of Mount Fuji. This was offensive to the Japanese, for the mountain is traditionally a place of pilgrimage.

Thirdly, the problem of military bases is related to moral problems. Prostitution has established itself near the bases with the resulting moral degradation and loss of human dignity and mutual respect in personal relations. The effect of such moral degradation to children and the community is incalculable. Here churches especially have an important task. The National Christian Council of Japan felt the responsibility to provide a wholesome environment and fellowship for American servicemen who have to serve their military duty far from their homes. Friendship Houses were created to minister to the spiritual and cultural needs of the men.

One of the most vital issues in which many Japanese find enthusiastic agreement is the stand against the use of and experiments with nuclear weapons. Granted that some of the opposition is adroitly cultivated by Communists, the intense feeling against the use and tests of atomic and hydrogen bombs is so widespread and genuine that it cannot be attributed merely to their influence. The Japanese Diet has twice unanimously passed resolutions calling for an end to A-bomb and H-bomb tests. It is reported that more than thirty-three million citizens have signed petitions to the same effect.

At the time of the Second Assembly of the World Council of Churches at Evanston, Illinois, the Japanese delegation proposed a resolution requesting prohibition of atomic and hydrogen bombs. The resolution was signed by 33,252 Japanese Christian young people. It helped to formulate the positive words regarding the issue in the report of the Assembly, which acknowledged the importance of the matter by calling for "the prohibition of all weapons of mass destruction including atomic and hydrogen bombs, with provision for international inspection and control, such as would safeguard the security of all nations, together with the drastic reduction of all other armaments."[3]

The test of the H-bomb in Bikini in the spring of 1954 strengthened the movement in Japan against nuclear tests. One of twenty-three Japanese fishermen died after being affected by radioactive fall-out from the Bikini bomb test. Recently the protests in Japan have centered on the tests that Great Britain made near Christmas Island in the Pacific.

The All Student Association in Japan has stood against the test of the nuclear bombs, and it was backed up by 250,000 students of 168 universities in 63 cities all over the country. Both the national student Y.M.C.A. and Y.W.C.A. have joined in appealing to the Chrisitan students in the world to work toward banning nuclear weapons and their testing.

Similar pronouncements have been formulated in major national bodies of Christian movements in Japan. The National Christian Council in its annual meeting in 1956 unanimously passed the following resolution:

"WHEREAS, Constant experiments in the Pacific and other areas have caused not only great and serious physical damage from the humanitarian point of view but also have endangered international good faith, be it

Resolved, That all world Christian agencies be called upon to create public opinion in all countries concerned for the discontinuance of such experiments."[4]

It should be pointed out that the Christian protest against the tests has been directed to Russia as well as to the United States and Great Britain, since this protest stems from religious and moral convictions rather than from sentimental emotions or political strategy. The protest is an expression of the sincere wish for the attainment of peace.

The effects of the 1945 bombings in Hiroshima and Nagasaki are still very much in the people's minds. According to John C. Bugher, Director of the United States Atomic Energy

Commission's Division of Biology and Medicine, the total number of dead from the two bombs was probably over 200,000, and most of those who survived suffered injuries. According to the report of the survey conducted in the spring of 1956 by the Atomic Bomb Patient Treatment Council of the United States Atomic Bomb Casualty Commission, out of the 110,000 survivors, 38,000 are now in need of treatment of some kind. Those who have actually been examined total only 7,700; of these, 1,439 were found to need treatment, yet only 732 have received it. The reason assigned was lack of funds. The government is now planning new legislation to provide funds for treatment and living expenses. Japanese Christian groups have been raising funds for this purpose.

One of the main reasons for protesting against the tests is the problem of contaminating fall-out. The Japanese scientists see as the main dangers infertility, the deposit in the body of strontium 90 that predisposes the victim to cancer, and the fact that a person's body can be damaged without his being aware of it. Since it is anticipated that people will increasingly be subject to radioactive effects through the peaceful use of atomic energy (its future use in medical treatment, for example), it is wise to limit the unnecessary increase of the radioactive element in the atmosphere in peacetime. This is still a much discussed and investigated problem among scientists in Japan. All, however, seem to agree in pointing out the dangers that the tests entail—dangers of lifelong damage to health or the appearance of serious hereditary defects. Then there is also the incalculable damage of the fear and international distrust created among the people in the areas where the tests are made.

Here it seems that wisdom and understanding should be united for the solution of the problem. For Japanese the issue should be taken up through reasonable and friendly persuasion of all people rather than an emotional and one-sided appeal to a particular country. On the other hand, the countries that insist on the tests should be aware of the urgent concern of many of those who have actually had the experience of atomic war and hydrogen bomb tests and should understand both the sensitivity of the people and the actual destructive effects that are possible as the result of the tests. Furthermore, the whole question should be dealt with more realistically through the creation of an authorized agency within the United Nations to control nuclear weapons under an effective inspection system in such a way as to eliminate and prohibit atomic, hydrogen, and all other weapons of mass destruction. Here the churches must promote international co-operation on the highest moral level. Christians in all nations face the vital task of lifting up international public opinion and thus carrying the real possibility of the reconciliation in Christ into the turmoil of international relations. In this whole area there is for Christians a deeply urgent need for a positive acceptance of the call of God to witness to the creative power of forgiveness and spiritual renewal.

CHAPTER SIX:

Concluding Reflections

As churches prepare to celebrate the one hundredth anniversary of Protestant missions in Japan in 1959, it is appropriate to reflect on the past course of Protestantism and to take a positive stand in relation to the future, responding to the challenges that the present places upon us. First of all, it is important to recognize that the Christian community in Japan has been and is a minority group. Including Roman Catholics, Eastern Orthodox, and Protestants, Christian forces are not more than 500,000, which is less than half of one per cent of the total population. This should not lead to an underestimation of the significance of the Christian churches in Japan. It indicates the need for co-operation among Protestant churches and underlines the importance of developing a positive program through which the churches as a creative minority can meet the challenge of modern Japan.

There is a need for a far wider dissemination of the Christian message in Japan. Until now the churches have been concentrated geographically in the large cities, and they have had their main influence among intellectuals. It is imperative now to bring the gospel to those who live in areas that Christianity has not yet strongly affected—to farmers in the rural areas and to workers in the industrial communities. This is a new and comparatively untried task for the church, a task that should be undertaken co-operatively with patience and courage by the total church. The more we understand the increasingly important role of working people in Japan, the more we recognize the vital meaning of this challenge to bring the gospel to workers in rural and industrial communities.

In general the Christian community in Japan still remains a part of Western Christianity. For the non-Christian ordinary folk, Christianity is still thought to be a Western and white man's religion, and there has been an undercurrent of antagonism toward Christianity that has existed continuously during the course of nationalistic expansion. In the fields of theology and church life, architecture, religious art, and hymns, Japanese Christians need to discover indigenous forms of expression. It is an encouraging sign that a growing interest in these things is being evinced among the Japanese churches.

A strong emphasis on the personal charismatic authority of outstanding persons has been characteristic of Christianity in Japan. Authority and respect were accorded the distinguished individual who had special gifts, talents, and ability. Churches tended to center upon the leadership of the minister, thus helping to establish an authoritarian pattern of human relationships. The church is a community of believers centering upon Jesus Christ who is the head of the Church. There is an urgent need in the Japanese church to clarify anew the meaning of the Church as the corporate body of Christ in the world and to come to understand the positive role of the layman with his responsibilities both in the church and in the world through and from the church.

Through education and an emphasis on self-discipline, Japanese Protestantism has made a valuable contribution to the pioneering efforts of social work and to the development of personal Christian character. As Japan moves in the direction of a complex modern society whose development is determined by the interaction of groups and organizations, it is of critical importance that Christian social concern now be expressed in an organized effort to deal with the causes of social evil and injustice rather than simply to alleviate the results. It is the task of the church not only to train people as good individual citizens with Christian character but also to urge upon them the necessity of their participation in a common effort to render a responsible Christian witness in a time of rapid social change.

In the face of far-reaching social transition, Christianity in Japan is confronted by the vital task of providing the moral basis for the establishment of a genuine sense of community. Formerly, in the old society, there was a strong emphasis on the supremacy of state and the freedom of the individual tended to be disregarded. In the postwar situation strong voices have been raised for the individual's rights, but responsibility toward the community has often been forgotten. The Christian church is challenged to demonstrate both the responsibility and the rights of persons in the midst of community and the necessity of responsible community as the place of individual fulfillment. The Church as the corporate body of Christ in society is the place for witness and demonstration of the Christian life. Against the notion of the isolated individual self or of the collective self, the church must affirm the Biblical doctrine of man, which asserts that man is created as a person-in-community, responsible to the love of God and called to love his neighbors in the church and in the wider community in which the Church exists.

The Japanese churches have been moving toward an increasing sense of unity as part of the corporate body of Christ. As part of the ecumenical movement, the churches have been reconsidering the nature of the church in theology and the development of forms of the organized church in practice. In this sense it was a significant fact that the United Church of Christ in Japan at its General Assembly in 1954 agreed upon a creed and established the Research Institute on the Mission of the Church. The creed was the first joint statement of their common Christian faith among the co-operating churches since the beginning of the United Church. The Research Institute was given the task of developing a unified program of study and investigation in five basic areas: theology of mission, method of evangelism, Christian education, church and society, and Christian international responsibility. This indicates the co-operative determination of these churches to find a firm Christian basis within the framework of the organized church from which to meet social problems, as over against the old basis of an individualistic liberal ideal. Furthermore, the increasing awareness among Protestant churches in Japan of the need for positive and corporate action in society has come with fuller participation in the world-wide Christian church and out of the conviction that Christ is indeed Lord over all of life.

Finally, as the world has been getting smaller through the technical development of the means of communication and transportation and in the light of the widespread wish for peace and fear of destruction, people have begun to realize more forcefully than ever before that we are living in one interdependent world. Moreover, through the development of the ecumenical movement, Christians in the world are called actively to strengthen the cause of mutual understanding and to increase better relations among the nations. It is obvious that no nation can be expected to act without consideration of its own national interest, its own safety, security, and well-being. But it is the responsibility of Christians to help the government and the people to conceive of the national interest in terms of the interdependence of nations in the modern world. With the enlarging of our understanding, we should see clearly that what ultimately serves the interests of the whole world community is also in the long run in the self-interest of our own country. It is important to recognize that communism cannot be overcome by mere military negation but by a deeper understanding and more constructive demonstration of concern for the human needs and welfare of all people.

One of the ironies of this interdependent small world is that the news we exchange is often bad news and the things we exchange often create misunderstanding and fear. When Japanese hear the announcement of the hydrogen bomb test, fear spreads among the majority of people. When Japan starts to reconstruct trade relations with the countries in Southeast Asia, misunderstanding and suspicion increase among those countries that were oppressed by the Japanese military during the war. When the United States Congress discusses the limitation of Japanese goods to be imported, there are serious fears of joblessness and hunger among the Japanese people. The wars we have experienced were certainly the worst example of such bad exchange.

There is an immeasurable need to bring the Good News that was proclaimed to all people through Jesus Christ. Christ who has brought reconciliation between God and the world is the source of our hope, calling us to the task of real reconciliation among persons, classes, races, and nations. There are urgent challenges on every hand to Christian churches throughout the world to increase mutual trust and establish better relations. Despite the dark outlook in the world, the Christian attitude toward this world responsibility is filled with a sense of joy and courage. It is a joyful endeavor to participate in the redemptive work of the risen Lord who has overcome all evil. It requires courage to accept the love of God in the world and courage to be a part of his creative and redemptive work through Christian churches. In accepting God's lordship over the world, it is the common responsibility of Christian churches throughout the world to respond with joy and courage and to commit themselves with new sincerity and effectiveness to the call of Christ, which is the call to reconciliation and renewal.

FOOTNOTES

Chapter One

1. *Niishima Jo,* by Yozo Yuasa, pp. 169-170.
2. *Danjo Ebina Sensei,* by Tsunekichi Watase, p. 112. Tokyo, 1938.
3. *Reminiscences of Seventy Years,* by Hiromichi Kozaki, p. 39. Tokyo.
4. *Ibid.,* p. 13.
5. "Kirisutokyo Judan Men," by Iwasaburo Okino, quoted in *Kindai Nihon no Keisei to Kirisutokyo,* by Mikio Sumiya, p. 35. Tokyo, 1950.

Chapter Three

1. "History of Socialism in Japan," by Kyokuzan Ishikawa and Shusui Kotoku, *Meiji Bunka Zenshu; Shakai Hen,* p. 380.
2. *Nihon Rodo Undo Shi,* by Eitaro Kishinoto, p. 40. Tokyo, 1950.
3. Quoted in *Reimeikino Nihon Rodo Undo,* by Kazuo Okochi, pp. 47-48. 1947.
4. *Twenty Years in the Labor Movement,* by Bunji Suzuki, pp. 54-55. Tokyo, 1931.
5. *The Japan Mission Year Book 1929,* pp. 127-128. Tokyo, Kyo Bun Kwan. Used by permission.
6. "The Conference on Factory Evangelism," by Akira Ebizawa, *The Japan Christian Year Book 1933.* Tokyo, Kyo Bun Kwan. Used by permission.

Chapter Four

1. *A New Theory of Politics and Religion,* by Hiromichi Kozaki, pp. 29-30. 1886.
2. Translation of the Rescript in *History of Christianity in Japan,* by Otis Cary, Vol. II, p. 226. Westwood, N. J., Fleming H. Revell & Company, 1909. Used by permission.
3. *Ibid.,* p. 227.
4. "The Future of Christianity in Japan," by Tokio Yokoi, *Rikugo Zasshi,* June, 1890.
5. "Christianity and Nationalism," by Hiromichi Kozaki, *Rikugo Zasshi,* June, 1890.

6. *Reminiscences of Seventy Years,* pp. 181-185.
7. *History of the Anti-War Movement in the Meiji and Taisho Periods,* by Yoshio Matsushito, p. 200. Tokyo, 1949.
8. *Zenshu,* by Kanzo Uchimura, Vol. XIV, p. 274. Tokyo, 1932.
9. *The Christian Movement in Japan, Korea, and Formosa,* pp. 138-139. Foreign Missions Conference, 1912.
10. *Zenshu,* by Masahisa Uemura, Vol. V, p. 231.
11. "State and Religion," by Daikichiro Tagawa, *Kokka to Shukyo,* p. 126.

Chapter Five

1. "The Christian Relief Program in Japan," by Esther B. Rhoads, *The Japan Christian Year Book 1950.* Tokyo, Kyo Bun Kwan, p. 133. Used by permission.
2. *Ibid.,* p. 135.
3. "Resolutions on International Affairs," *Evanston Report,* edited by W. A. Visser 't Hooft, p. 146. New York, Harper and Brothers, 1955. Used by permission.
4. *Japan Christian Activity News,* Commission on Public Relations of the National Christian Council of Japan, April 15, 1956.

Other Friendship Press publications on Japan are available through Friendship Press or denominational literature headquarters.

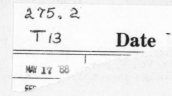
Manufactured by Sowers Printing Company
Cover printed by Affiliated Lithographers
Format designed by Dorothy Papy
Binding by Louise E. Jefferson